A RESOURCE FOR STUDYING SCRIPTURE AND
A COMPANION FOR TRAVELING IN

THE LANDS OF THE BIBLE (Volume 2)

IN THE FOOTSTEPS OF PAUL AND JOHN:

VISITING SITES IN:

- GREECE,
- THE GREEK ISLANDS AND
- WESTERN TURKEY

GERALD L. BORCHERT

In the Footsteps of Paul and John

Gerald L. Borchert, PhD (Princeton Theological Seminary), LLB (University of Alberta Law School), was Seminary Dean and Professor of New Testament (twice retired) and is currently Senior Professor at Carson Newman College. Dr. Borchert was also Thesis Director for the Robert E. Webber Institute for Worship Studies.

Mossy Creek Press
121 Holly Trail Road, NW
Cleveland, Tennessee 37311

The Lands of the Bible (Volume 2) In the Footsteps of Paul and John: Visiting Sites in Greece, The Greek Islands and Western Turkey.

© 2012 by Gerald L. Borchert. All rights reserved. Published 2012.

Printed in the United States of America.

ISBN 978-1-936912-63-6

No part of this book may be reproduced or transmitted in any form or by any means, electronic or mechanical, including photocopying, recording, or by information storage and retrieval system, without permission in writing from the publisher.

To order additional copies of this book, contact:

Mossy Creek Press
1-423-475-7308

www.mossycreekpress.com

CONTENTS

Preface   5

Chapter 1: General Introduction   9

    A. Dating and Archaeological Periods
    B. The Seven Ecumenical Councils
    C. The Use of Terms
       Myth, Tradition
    D. The Pantheon
    E. An Overview of this Work
    F. The Roman Empire and its Changes

Chapter 2: Visiting the Mainland of Greece   17

    A. Northern Greece – Macedonia
       Philippi; Neapolis; Amphipolis; Apollonia; Mount Athos;
       Thessaloniki/Saloniki/Thessalonica;
       Mount Olympus; Beroea/Berea/Veria; Vergina/Aigai.
    B. Central Greece
       Meteora/Kalambaka; Delphi/Delfi.
    C. Athens and the Immediate Area of Attica
       Athens
    D. The Cities of the Peloponnese
       Corinth, Mycenae/Mykine/Mycene; Epidaurus; Olympia; Sparta.

Chapter 3: Visiting the Greek Islands   49

    A. Departing the Mainland
       Piraeus.
    B. The Cyclades Islands, Part 1
       Mykonos; Delos.
    C. The Dodecanes Islands
       Patmos; Rhodes/Rodos and Lindos.
    D. Crete/Kriti
       Heraklion.
    E. The Cyclades Islands, Part 2
       Santorini/Thira.

In the Footsteps of Paul and John

Chapter 4: Visiting Western Turkey/Anatolia — 59

  A. Ephesus; The Leading City of Ancient Asia and Its Close Neighbors
Kusadasi; Ephesus; Ayasoluk/Selcuk.

  B. Istanbul and its Environs: The Ancient-Modern Metropolis
Byzantium/Constantinople/Istanbul.

  C. Touching Western Bithyinia
Chalcedon/Kadikoy; Nicomedia/Izmit; Nicea/Iznick.

  D. Moving South through Ancient Mysia
Bursa/Prusa; Balikesir.

  E. Circling Around the Churches of Revelation
    1. Part I - The First Three Churches
Thyatira/Akhisar; Smyrna/Izmir; Inserting Ephesus (See Section A).
    2. Three Neartby Sites
Priene/Gullubace; Miletus/Milet/Balet; Aphrodisias/Afrodisias/Geyre.
    3. Part II - The Last Four Churches
The Tri-cities of Laodicea/Eskihisar; Colossae/Honaz and Hierapolis/Pamukkala; Philadelphia/Alasehir; Sardis/Sart; Pergamum/Bergama;

  F. The Vacinity of Ancient Troy
Assos/Behramkalle; Troas/Alexander Troas/Dalyan; Troy/Truva/Trevfikiye; Canakkale.

Chapter 5: Some Helpful Information for Traveling to Greece and Turkey — 103

*Passports & Visas, Hotels, Guides & Drivers,
Medium of Exchange/Currencies, Protection of Money & Valuables
Electricity, Dress, Packing/Luggage, Cameras
Food, Beverages & Water, Shopping, Schedules/Time*

A Brief Bibliography — 107

Pictures: — 109

  A. From the Greek Mainland
  B. From the Greek Islands
  C. From Western Turkey

Index to Places and Pictures — 133

Index to Area and Site Maps — 136

PREFACE

An historical and geographical resource for the study of Scripture and a companion for visiting the Lands of the Bible is an indispensable tool for the Christian. But even more significant is a pilgrimage involving a Seminar in which one is actually able to study and visit the Bible Lands in person. As Christians we can be greatly enriched by becoming better acquainted with the actual places which are part of our spiritual heritage. These places can become for us significant witnesses to the events that changed forever the course of history. What happened in the Lands of the Bible has become important in the history of humanity and it should be extremely significant to each one who has taken the name of Jesus, the Christ.

As you consider these lands and – one hopes – you are able to travel in the footsteps of Paul and John, may you gain a new sense of vitality as you relive the journeys when these early Christians faced hostile crowds, were beaten, imprisoned and without backing down did their ministries with a commitment inspired by the divine presence of God's Spirit in their lives. May you be reminded that the churches in these regions were birthed in one of the most difficult and yet exciting periods of history when the Gospel message first burst onto the world's scene. In this part of the world some of these churches have continued with vitality while others have lost their zeal and still others have faded into the past and only archaeological ruins are now left to mark places where vibrant congregations once met and served Christ as Lord. But almost all of these ancient congregations suffered persecution for their Lord. Some were also part of the intense theological task of seeking to define who Jesus Christ really is and in so doing they staked their reputations and lives on his divinity, resurrection and Lordship.

I have listed in the first chapter the seven early Eumentical Councils where the early Christians tried to hammer out the contents of what should compose the core of the Christian faith. Not everyone agreed with the decions that were forthcoming from them but they began the hard task of trying to discern what was "orthodox" or correct theology. Even today many Christians do not agree with all the decisions that were made and so the wrestling continues because as Emile Calliet of Princeton used to say: "It is difficult to colonize the reality with the intelligible." Or to put it another way: Ultimate reality, namely God, does not fit into the teacups of our minds! But we all struggle to understand such reality and we often manufacture "god" or "gods" in our own image. Such is the history of the world. The early people struggled to understand God and so they made many "gods" and I have listed some of the Greek and Roman gods of the Pantheon because, as Luther and others have said, humans will have "entweder Gott order Abgott." They will have either God or an idol. And as humans get in the way of other humans, we fight for property which we assume belongs to us -- or we suppose should belong to us. Accordingly, this study will include a rehersal of how often these lands and cities have changed hands and become the "possessions" of others only to find that the property is wrested from one set of hands for another in a few years and new gods or the same gods with new names are graciously honored for assistance in vicious conquests. As you read this book, and hopefully visit these lands, do not simply move from place to place as non-perceptive tourists who do not reflect on the historical significance of what you see or read but please consider seriously the implications of what history and lands can teach us about ourselves and about others.

Welcome then to this little study in which together we will consider some of the lands of the early church and the pagan or mythical contexts in which the dieiies were served. Even more, I pray that you will have the wonderful opportunity to walk in the footsteps of these two great proclaimers of the Gospel as I have done on many occasions. But I want you to remember that the early church did not enter this earthly sphere perfect (just think about the Corinthian Christians and their poblems), nor was the church born in a vacuum (consider Paul's preaching in Athens). The lands of Greece and Asia Minor are ancient lands where cultures have risen and fallen over the millennia. Therefore, I have purposely not merely confined my discussions to the various sites mentioned in the New Testament but I have sought to help you the reader to understand the contextual framework out of which the Roman Empire developed. The Romans were basically syncretists which meant that they, like almost all people, borrowed from what was good in other cultures. You will quickly note that I have sought to provide brief historical background notes on many of these places so that the reader would be able to understand the various settings where the Good News of Jesus was powerfully proclaimed. And I have purposely not stopped with Paul and John but Ihave sought to indicate the history beyond their time as well. I have also included information on places that are not mentioned in the New Testament because those sites are crucial for an adequate understanding of the places where the Gospel took root and also has nearly died.

I have always taught my students that understanding the Greco-Roman world is crucial for gaining a fuller perception of our biblical records and the history of the Christian Church. The places I mention should be on the minds if not the itineraries of people who visit the Lands of the Bible. Understanding those contexts should hopefully provide new insights for a more adequate application of the Gospel to our contexts and ministries.

It should naturally be noted here that I have not been able to give the reader the full details on all the sites which are mentioned because of the nature of this little book nor have I included all the places which I have visited in this part of the world during my past forty plus years of traveling in theses lands. But this little work, like my earlier one which covers Israel, Egypt and the Sinai, Jordan, Syria and Lebanon (as well as the Palestinian Territories and notes on Islam), proposes to be a handbook or a brief handy companion to the northeastern Mediterranean basin for those who might wish to travel in that region of the world and for those who would desire a helpful supportive tool in the study of the Bible.

As in the case of all prefaces, it is important to mention those who have been significant to an author in producing his work. I must here mention the many guides who have helped me understand their lands better and for whom I may have added a little to their knowledge from my years of study and instruction at the feet of eminent biblical scholars in North America and Europe. I am indebted to all of them but I take full responsibility for any errors that I may have made in the process of producing this little work. It goes without saying that we continue to learn from the research work of others and from the continual archaeological discoveries that are being made. They help us to refine our earlier ideas and force us to read constantly on this important subject in order that we might provide the best insights for students and lay people into the Bible and its background studies.

I am also indebted particularly to the multiple tour agents who have helped me in my journeys. Particularly would I acknowledge Educational Opportunities and its leaders Jim and his son James Ridgeway and their staff. Also, I must mention Bible Lands/Dehoney Travel and its leaders the late Wayne Dehoney and his daughter Kathy Evitts and their staff. In Turkey I would likewise mention Tutku Tours with Levant Oral and his staff. All of these organizations have been exemplary and have gone out of their way to adjust itineraries even late in the processes to suit my purposes of giving Christian pilgrims the best insights into the Lands of the Bible. I also acknowledge the government travel offices in the various countries and others who have supplied me with travel information and maps. I have clipped and enhanced many of these sources and used them with permission to assist the reader and traveler. I would also note that I have made an effort to assist the reader in **the identification of places by putting Numbers and Small Letters in bold face** at the start of the descriptions and I have coordinated them with numbers on the maps and with the "Index to Places and Picutres" in the back of the book. I have also supplied an "Index to Area and Site Maps." The 113 pictures near the back of the book which I have taken over a number of years should not only stimulate interest but also help as a reminded of the sites visited. I acknowledge that a handful of pictures were supplied to me by a couple of people who have traveled with me on my journeys to these biblical lands and I express my thanks to them.

I must also add a deep gratitude for my dear wife who has suffered my many hours of studying and writing in my study and endured my scores of trips to the Mediterranean world. Fortunately in recent years she has been able to join me much of the time and once again I gladly dedicate this little work to her.

Finally, to the Triune God I give thanks daily for the opportunities that I have been given to study and to teach the biblical texts for more than half a century in many parts of the world including those lands where the Gospel first took firm root and as it moved beyond the Mediterranean basin to the far reaches of the earth. To God be the Glory!

Gerald L. Borchert, Ph. D., LL.B.

(For a brief resume of the author, please see the last page of this work)

CHAPTER 1

GENERAL INTRODUCTION

Ever since I became a Christian the lives of Paul and John have always exerted a phenomenal influence on me because I have been convinced that they sought to follow in the footsteps of Jesus just as Peter wrote that we as Christians should seek to follow in the steps of our Lord (1 Pet 3:21). The writings which have been linked to these two servants of Jesus compose a large percentage of the New Testament and like all the writers of the Christian canon they summon Christians of every generation to join in an authentic imitation of Christ (cf. Phil 2:5; 3:17; 1 John 4:7-11). Of course, following in the footsteps of Paul and John in the New Testament does not mean to walk on the streets where they walked or to touch the stones which they touched but it implies to live like they lived, copying Jesus through the power of the Holy Spirit.

Nevertheless, there is something quite special about visiting the Lands of the Bible and reflecting on the places where these two early missionaries of Christ did in fact work and even more to ponder at these sites the influence these missionaries have had upon the entire world as a result of following Jesus. In this brief work, therefore, I trust that you will sense that my goal is to help you as a Christian to remember that when we think about these lands and especially when we visit them, we are not merely doing so as tourists but as pilgrims who prayerfully seek to encounter God in relation to these places.

Now in this work, I will refer to a number of details and terms which require some further explanation and understanding and so I will herewith briefly review a few matters that I have discussed more at length in my first volume on *The Lands of the Bible*.[1]

A. DATING AND ARCHAEOLOGICAL PERIODS

First, I would remind you that archaeologists and historians have divided our understanding of time into various periods. The periods overlap when you move from country to country but a general understanding of these periods can be helpful in our task of reflection. The dates below are generalities and while they are normally used in reference to the Lavant or the area of Israel and its neighbors, I have here made some adjustments for the Northeastern Mediterranean world.

---

[1] See Gerald L. Borchert, *The Lands of the Bible: Israel, The Palestinian Territories, Sinai and Egypt, Jordan, Notes on Syria and Lebanon, Comments on the Arab-Israeli Wars and the Palestinian Refugees, The Clash of Cultures* (Cleveland TN, 2011), 6-14.

In the Footsteps of Paul and John

Old Stone Age	Prior to 10,000 BC
Middle Stone Age	10,000 to 8,000 BC
Late Stone Age (Neolithic)	8,000 to 4,500 (or 4,000) BC
Copper/Bronze-Stone Age (Chalcolithic)	4,500 to 3,150 BC
Early Bronze Age	3,200 to 2,200 BC
Middle Bronze Age	2,200 to 1,550 BC
Minoan Period	2000 to 1450 BC
Mycenaean Period	1700 to 1100 BC
Late Bronze Age	1,550 to 1,200 BC (some date it to 1050 BC in Greece)
(Early Iron Age	1,200 to 950 BC)
(Middle Iron Age	950 to 586 BC)
Geometric Period in Greece	1050 to 700 BC
(Archaic Period in Greece	c. 700 to c.489 BC)
Solon's Reforms to Pericles in Athens	594 to 420 BC
Late Iron Age (Babylonian/Persian Period)	586 to 333 BC
Hellenistic Age (Alexander and Macedon)	333 to 168/63 BC
Battle of Pydna and the Early Roman Period in Greece	168 BC to AD 324
Battle of Actium/Beginning of the Roman Empire	31ff. BC
Byzantine Age (new capital Constantinople)	AD 324/25 to 1354-1453 (to 636 in Israel)
(Islamic Period in Israel	AD 636 to 1917)
Fall of Constantinople & Early Muslim Period	AD 1354 to 1453
Ottoman Rule	AD 1453 to 1821 (in Greece) to 1922 (in Turkey)
Struggle for Independence in Greece	AD 1821 to 1830
Domination of Greece by European Powers	AD 1830 to 1967
The Turkish Republic	AD 1923 to the present
Unrest and the Demise of the Monarchy in Greece	AD 1968 to 1974
The Greek Republic	AD 1975 to the present

B. THE SEVEN ECUMENICAL COUNCILS[2]

Christians who travel throughout Greece and Turkey should be aware of the seven Ecumenical Councils that sought to hammer out the elements of the Christian faith. Early theologians of the Church sought to be precise in their thinking about the coming of Christ and the implications of salvation and even proceeded to the point of declaring the legitimacy of icons and statues. The bishops of the Church were not always kind to those with whom they disagreed and they frequently condemned and excommunicated each other from the Church as they understood it. For their tenacity in seeking clarity concerning the faith we should b grateful. But concerning their unkindness and harshness to each other in asserting their own views and rational formulas of the faith we should be forewarned against following in those footsteps.

The First Council (AD 325) was convened by Emperor Constantine at Nicea to deal with the two fold nature of Christ. It rejected Arianism (the Son was not eternal and had a beginning).

The Second Council (381) was convened by Emperor Theodosius at Constantinople to clarify the earlier Nicene Confession and enunciate the divinity of the Holy Spirit while rejecting again Arianism and adding the rejection of Appolinarianism (Christ had two separate natures).

The Third Council (431) was convened by Emperor Theodosius II at Ephesus to assert the theology of Mary as the *theotokos* ("bearer of God") over against Nestorius while also rejecting the view of Pelagius on "original sin" (everyone at birth had the right to choose good).

The Fourth Council (451) was convened by Emperor Marcian at Chalcedon after an earlier council in 449 at Ephesus had refused to listen to Leo I of Rome but this great council with six hundred bishops present solemnly declared that the inseparable 2 natures of the divine and the human existed in Jesus Christ and it rejected the views of Eutyches that Jesus Christ was *homousion* (of one nature) only with the Father. The result was the Nicene Creed.

The Fifth Council (553) was convened by Emperor Justinian at Constantinople which reaffirmed both the two full natures of Jesus Christ and rejected Monophysitism (the divine nature of Christ transformed his human nature and so Jesus Christ became divine).

The Sixth Council (680) was convened by Emperor Constantine IV in Constantinople which reaffirmed again the two natures of Jesus Christ and refused to accept Monothelitism which sought to distinguish between the two wills of Christ.

The Seventh Council (787) was convened by Emperor Constantine VI in Nicea which officially authorized the veneration of icons and statues in the Church. It rejected the early iconoclastic movement but such veneration was again raised during the Protestant Reformation.

---

[2] For further information see Henry Bettenson, *Documents of the Christian Church* (London, New York, etc.: Oxford University Press, 1944, etc.) and the classic work of Kenneth Scott Latourette, *A History of Christianity* (New York: Harper & Brothers, 1953).

C. THE USE OF TERMS

"Myth": I have referred to the Greek myths frequently in discussing the ancient sites and I need to emphasize that I use the term "myth" in a technical sense which includes not only the concept of legend but more importantly it refers to a story or tale that seeks to define a reality which was hard for the ancients to explain. The Greek myths, thus, are attempts to interpret historical and metaphysical realities in terms of anthropological and physical phenomena which can be recognized by our five senses. They often involve divine and semi-divine like figures who are engaged in activities, foibles and events that are interpreted as providing meaning and explanation for the existence of these historical and metaphysical realities to which they refer.

These myths should by no means be treated as insignificant or lacking in meaning by people of our generation. They are not only significant but they contain genuine reflections of authentic realities from the past. For example, most scholars once regarded the stories of Homer in the *Iliad* and the *Odyssey* to be merely fanciful, created tales by the famous poetic writer until Heinrich Schliemann decided to use the stories of Homer to try and locate the lost ancient city of Troy. To everyone's surprise he not only located it but he also found the riches that he believed would have been buried there. The same can be said for his uncovering of the city of Mycenae.

I would encourage my readers not to avoid this literature but when they have a little spare time to peruse some of these Greek myths because they have some rather intriguing moral lessons to communicate to us. Of course, I am not here suggesting that centaurs (half man and half horse) and the Minotaur (a half man and half bull monster) actually existed or that an early Athenian king was in fact a half human and half snake. But I am suggesting that we ought to ask why the ancients thought the serpent was an important symbol and why that symbol persisted to have meaning for them.

"Tradition": I also use the term tradition in a technical sense. We may not be sure about whether a site is the actual place that an event occurred but over the course of centuries people have come to associate particular places/sites with particular events. The development of such traditions is usually the result of people seeking to make spiritual pilgrimages to remember the person and/or event associated with a place. But the actual place may not be known. Now like many archaeologists and researchers we do our research with a view to determining the authenticity of sites not only for the academy but also for people on journeys like those who visit the Lands of the Bible. Genuine scholars do not normally tell people that a site is the actual place where an event took place unless they are fairly sure of their facts. Naturally new evidence may become available to change an older view but the goal is to give our best considered opinion at the time concerning such matters.

Events that are mentioned in the Bible are important to people and pilgrimages are experiences of visiting places that allow people to reflect on those events. When we are not sure that a site visited is the actual place an event took place or when we recognize that a site visited is not likely to be the original site of the event then we designate that site as traditional. In the land of Israel there are many such sites which have been preserved through the centuries by the building of chapels over those sites in order to preserve the memories of the earlier events. Many such sites were chosen primarily because they were accessible. But Israel is not the only place where there are traditional sites. Such traditional Christian sites are also present in Greece and Turkey.

If we take Philippi as an example, it is impossible to say where Lydia (the Lydian woman) was baptized. There are several possible sites for the baptism but the little site (known as the Baptistery of St. Lydia) near the Krenides stream/creek and the western gate where there is in a little park probably appeals to the psyches of most Protestants. It certainly could have been the actual site. But now contrast that site with the cistern that has been designated as the prison where Paul and Silas were placed prior to their hearing. Everything about that site, from a historian's point of view, seems to be wrong. It is virtually in the center of the old city, near the Egnatian highway and the grand theater and it was probably too small for what would have been the city prison. Yet it is in a convenient place for later pilgrims to visit after the city lay in ruins. Remembering that in spite of the fact that Paul and Silas had been harassed and were thrown into prison to compensate for the loss of someone else's unjust revenues that they were still able to sing and pray is a worthy spiritual practice to be emulated. Connecting that event to the supposed traditional site marked for the event is, however, not a necessity or even a probability.

D. THE PANTHEON AND MYTHICAL FIGURES

(Some of the Greek and Roman Mythical Deities)

The Union of *Chronos* (Time/Sky) with *Gea/Rhea* (Earth/Matter) provided the Greeks with their foundational "Myth of Creation."

The Twelve Olympian Gods

Zeus –Jupiter/Jove (cf. Baal in the Semitic lands): King, the god of Thunder and Storms. He had many mistresses like Leto and Europa. (See Thessaloniki/Mount Olympus &Crete)

Hera-Juno (cf. The Isis Mystery in Egypt): Queen

Apollo (Helios): Sun, Prophecy, Music, Poetry (See especially Delphi)

Ares-Mars: War, Power (cf. to Michael in the Bible)

Hermes-Mercury: Messenger (cf. to Gabriel in the Bible)

Poseidon-Neptune: The Sea (See Athens)

Hephaistos-Vulcan: Fire and Metal Working

Athena-Minerva: Wisdom (See Athens) regarded as a virgin

Aphrodite-Venus: Love and Beauty (See especially Corinth)

Artemis-Diana: Huntress, Moon goddess, Productivity (See: Ephesus) regarded as a virgin

Demeter-Ceres: Agriculture (who together with Zeus birthed Persephone – cf. the union of Baal with Ashteroth)

Hestia-Vesta: The Home/Hearth, Domestic Matters, regarded as a virgin

Other Mythical Deities and Figures

Pluto-Dis/Hades: Underworld

Persephone: Daughter of Zeus and Demeter who was abducted by Pluto/Hades

Dionysus –Bacchus: Wine and Revelry

Asclepius: Healing, Medicine (Deified by Zeus; See especially Epidaurus)

Janus: Roman Doors, Gates

Pan (half-human/goat): Shepherd and Hunter

Minotaur (half-human/bull): Evil Extortionist (See Heraklion, Crete)

Centaur (half-human/horse): Good and Wise Teacher of the Healing Art to Asclepius

E. AN OVERVIEW OF THE CONTENTS OF THIS WORK

It is now important to provide a brief overview of the major sites that should be on the various itineraries which Christians use in following the footsteps of Paul and John. As indicated earlier, not all the places mentioned in this work were visited by the missionaries but all of these places are important for gaining an understanding of the background and context to the world in which the Gospel was sent during the opening era of the Christian Church.

We begin our analysis in this work with Macedonia, the country of Philip II and his renowned son, Alexander the Great (hereafter *Alexander G*). The first city discussed is Philippi, named after Philip II and its seaport of Neapolis. From there we move to Amphipolis and Apollonia and end our journey on the ancient Egnatian highway with Thessaloniki (Thessalonica) where Paul was said to have turned the world pattern on its head. In this journey we bypass Mount Athos, the site of many famous monasteries. Thessaloniki is today Greece's second largest city and from here on a clear day one can often see Mount Olympus, the sanctuary of the gods. We then turn southwest touching Beroea before stopping at the royal Macedonian city of Vergina (ancient Aigai) and the burial site of Philip II. The next stage is south and a visit to the spectacular monasteries built on rock fingers at Meteora followed by a visit to the most sacred Greek shrine city of Delphi. We then finally reach Athens, the philosophic and artistic center of Achaia which is today Greece's largest city. Our final section on the mainland of Greece is our journey to Corinth (the Roman capital) and the

Peloponnese with the historic city of Mycenae and the shrine city of Epidaurus. Some tours will stop at Olympia the shrine city of Zeus as well as other gods and the famous athletic center of Greece that gave birth to the Olympic Games. But very few tour groups visit Sparta in the south because not much is today visible.

The second major section of our pilgrimage is by ship to some of the magnificent Greek islands. It begins at Piraeus, the seaport of Athens. The first stop is at the vacation center of Mykonos, which is also the staging site for a visit to the the significant shrine island of Delos for those who have the time to visit it. From Mykonos the next stop may be Ephesus on some tours but we shall leave that information for our discussion of Western Turkey/Anatolia/Asia Minor. Instead, we will move to Patmos where John received his vision for the Book of Revelation. From there we will stop at the beautiful island of Rhodes famous for the Colossus which fell during an earthquake but in its place today one can visit the gigantic Crusader's fortress and enjoy shopping in the many small shops that line the streets. And one should not miss the magnificent acropolis at Lindos which overlooks the traditional site of St. Paul's Harbor. The next stop is at the island of Crete and its ancient capital of Knossos which was the seat of the Minoan culture with its legends about Zeus and the Minotaur. Finally, we land at Santorini, certainly one of the most picturesque islands in the world and the site of one of the most shattering volcanic explosions in history that may have been instrumental in the ending of great Minoan culture.

The third section of this little book involves a visit to Turkey and the cities listed by John in his letters to the churches in Revelation including not only Ephesus, one of most interesting archaeological sites in the world but also Izmir (Smyrna), the third largest city in Turkey. Also, of strategic significance is the magnificient acropolis of Pergamum and the ruins of ancient Sardis. Thiatira and Philadelphia are not as fruitful in terms of visiting but the tri-cities of Hierapolis/Laodicea/Colossae are exceedingly interesting. Hierapolis is a UNESCO city with its calcified cliffs and great ruins. Laodicea is slowly being uncovered but not much can be seen at Colaossae. The nearby ancient city of Aphrodisias, however, is one of the great archaeological sites in Turkey. Along the coast one should consider Miletus and its neighboring town of Priene with the Temple of Athena. The itinerary should by all means include the historic sites at Truva (ancient Troy and later Alexanader Troas and its neighboring town of Assos). And, of course, Istanbul the great city of Constantine (Constantinople), ancient Byzantium, is one of the most interesting cities in the world. Other important sites near Istanbul include Chalcedon, Nicomedia and Nicea, all important in the Byzantine Period. In moving south one also comes to Bursa, the early capital of the Ottoman Empire and one can overnight in other towns such as Balikesir. God bless you as you travel throughout this part of the world and may history come alive to you!

F. THE ROMAN EMPIRE AND ITS CHANGES:

From the Julius Caesar (44 BC) to Augustus and Hadrian (AD117)

From Justinian

AD 527-565

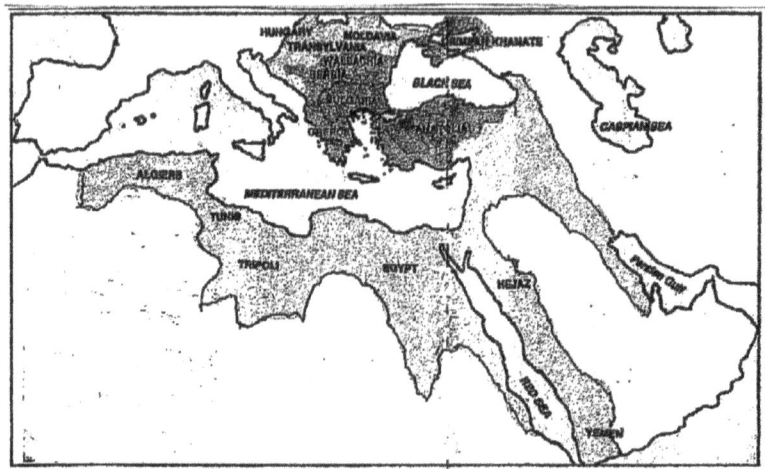

The Ottoman Empire from

Suleiman the Magnificent

AD 1520-1566

CHAPTER 2

VISITING THE MAINLAND OF GREECE

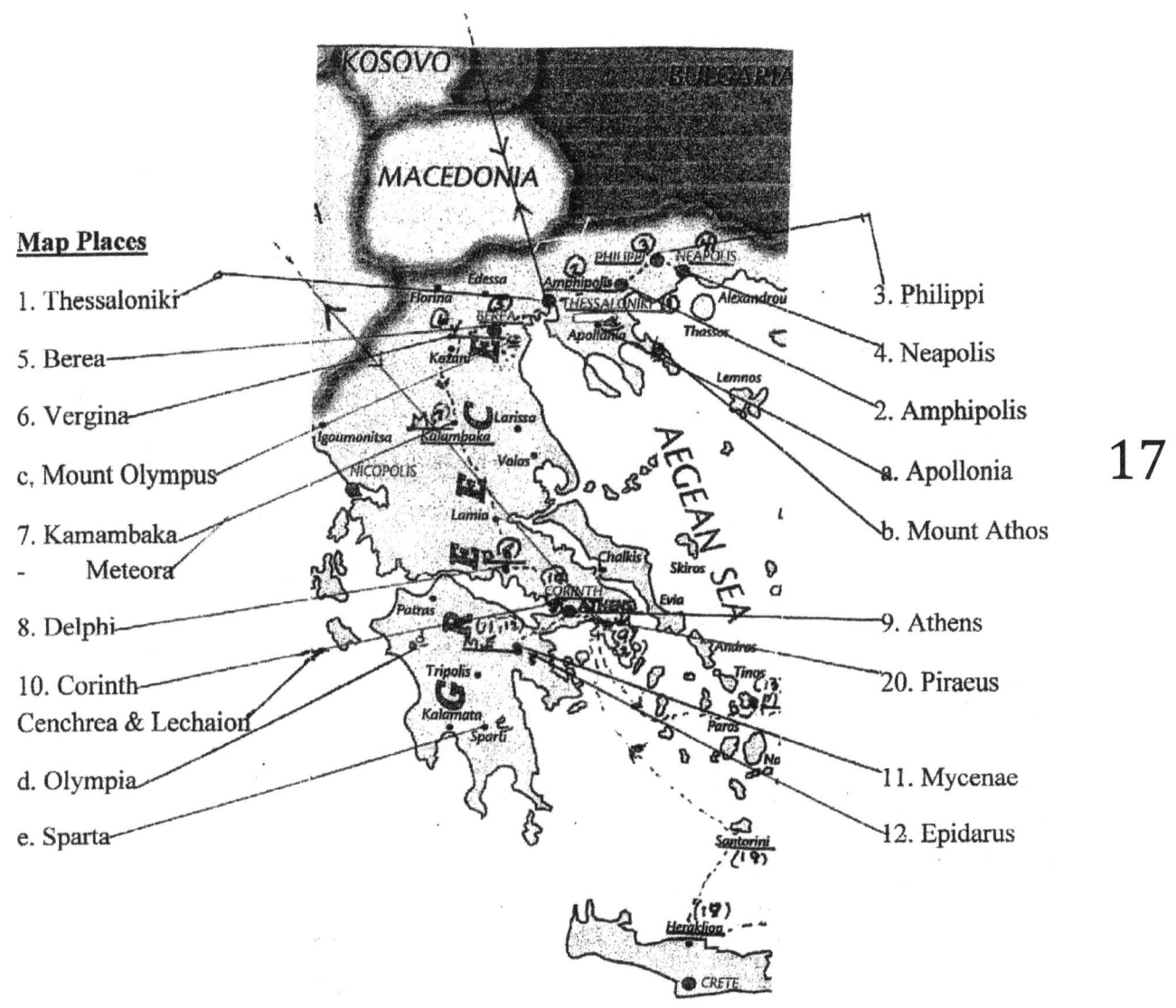

Map Places

1. Thessaloniki
5. Berea
6. Vergina
c. Mount Olympus
7. Kamambaka
   - Meteora
8. Delphi
10. Corinth
    Cenchrea & Lechaion
d. Olympia
e. Sparta

3. Philippi
4. Neapolis
2. Amphipolis
a. Apollonia
b. Mount Athos
9. Athens
20. Piraeus
11. Mycenae
12. Epidarus

A. NORTHERN GREECE- MACEDONIA

Philippi[3]: **(3)**[4] The city is located at the foot of Mt. Pangaion (Pangaeum) in a plain which extends to the northwest that in ancient times was quite swampy but has in recent times been drained and is now very productive for growing grains, fruits and vegetables. Since the area is surrounded by hills and mountains it became a strategic military center but its significance was greatly enhanced by the fact that **gold** was discovered in the hills near Philippi. Warriors from the nearby island of **Thasos**, under the leadership of the exiled Athenian politician Calistratus, seized the territory and founded their city of **Krenides** ("springs") near to the site of Philippi.

When **Philip II**, the father of Alexander the Great (hereafter *Alexander G*), gained the throne of Macedon, he realized the strategic significance of the site, captured it, rebuilt it, fortified it with walls, populated it with Macedonians, and renamed it after himself. The veins of gold were vigorously mined and during the reigns of both Philip and *Alexander G* they provided the resources for paying their military forces (Diodorus xvi. 8). The entire area was seized by the Romans after the **Battle of Pydna** (just south of Thessaloniki) in 168 BC and the Roman consul, L. Aemilius Paullus, divided Macedonia into 4 districts, the first included Philippi with Amphipolis being chosen as the capital. The gold was soon exhausted and Strabo (vii. 331) indicated that Philippi shrunk in size "to a small settlement."

[See Pictures # 1 a & b. – The Bema near the Via Egnatia in the Philippi Forum]

That situation might have continued if had not been for a twist in history. On the plains of Philippi in 42 BC, following the **murder of Julius Caesar**, Brutus and Cassius (the assassins) were finally defeated in battle with **Mark Antony and Octavian.** In honor of the victory the city was given the status of a Roman Colony with the rights of Rome (*Coloni Victrix Philippensium*). The defeated army was banished from Rome and was divested of property in Italy (Dio Cassius li. 4) and as a result many of the soldiers settled in Philippi. While Antony was the major victor in the battle, his alignment with **Cleopatra** alienated him from his loyal soldiers and in the subsequent face-off between Antony and Octavian the forces of Antony and Cleopatra were solidly defeated at **Actium** in 31 BC. As a result more defeated soldiers settled in Philippi. Octavian who then was honored with the special designation as **"Augustus"** also redesignated the city as *Coloni Augusta Iulia (Victrix) Philippensium.* The victory at Actium was a major political turning point because: (1) it defined Augustus as the rightful successor to Caesar, and (2) it ended the Roman Republic and began the new era of the Roman Empire by giving Augustus supreme power – the real quest of Julius Caesar.

Philippi is mentioned in Acts 16; 20:6; Phil 1:1; 1 Thess2:2 and implied in 2 Cor 8:1 and Phil 4:15, as a strategic city near the eastern end of the Macedonian section on the **Egnatian** highway (*Via Egnatia*) which traversed the Balkan peninsula (northern Greece) and linked the Adriatic Sea on the

---

[3] For more information on this site see G. L. Borchert, "Philippi" in *The International Standard Bible Encyclopedia*, rev. ed., Vol. 3 (Grand Rapids: Eerdmans, 1986), 834-36.

[4] The bold numbers and small letters in brackets conform to the numbers on the maps and the numbers before the discussions of each place/city/island in this book.

west with the Roman provinces in Asia Minor on the east. While this major road continued east beyond Macedonia into the wilds of ancient Thrace which was infested with bandits, travelers like **Paul** tended to end and begin their overland journeys on the highway at Philippi's seaport of **Neapolis** (modern Kavalla) which is about 10 miles (16 km.) to the south.

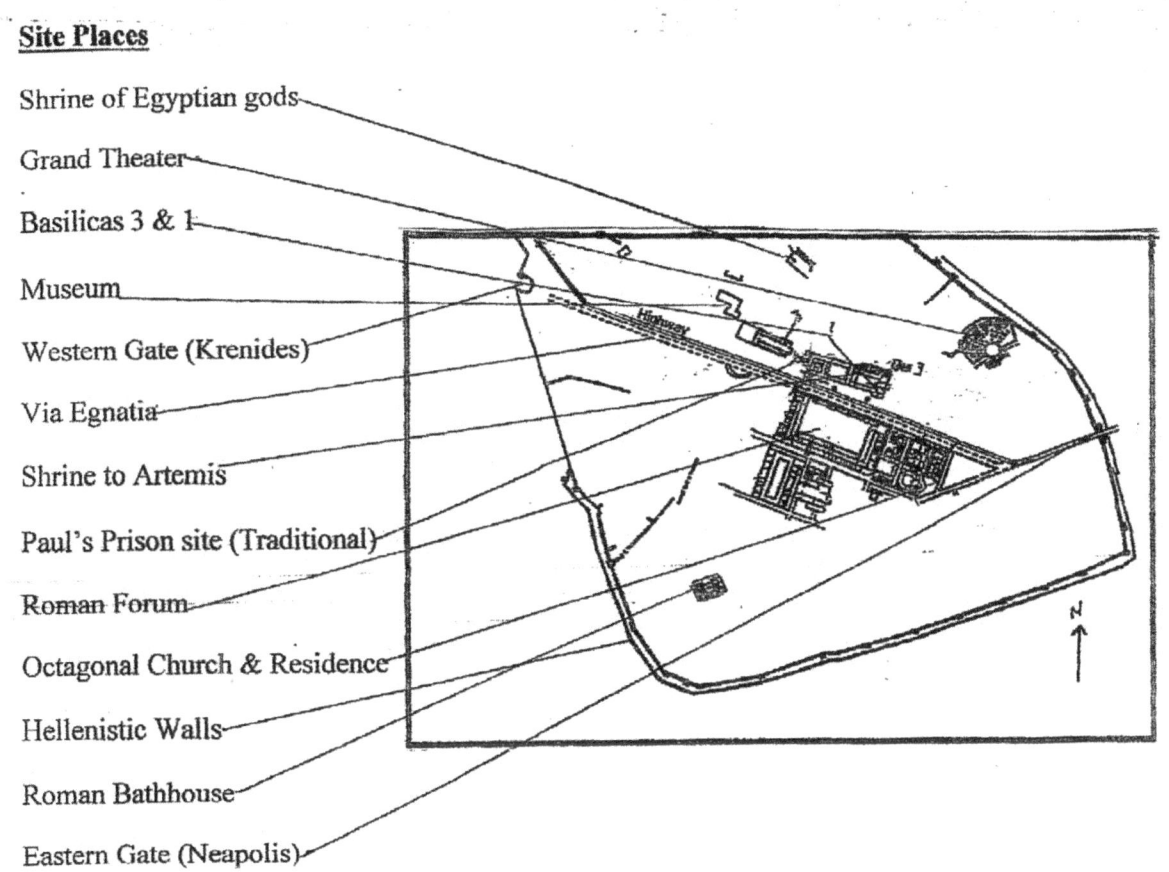

Site of Ancient Philippi

At the time (c. AD 49) **Paul, Silas (Silvanus), Luke and Timothy** visited Philippi and Christian missionary work spread from Asia to Europe (cf. Acts 16:9ff.), the city was flourishing and despite the fact that Amphipolis remained the capital of the district, Philippi grew as an independent **colony** and the center of activity in eastern Macedonia. Although the settlers in Philippi may have been banished veterans, the loyalty to Rome of these displaced settlers was well known and Luke mirrors that view in the charge against Paul that he was teaching practices that were not permitted by law for "us Romans" to follow (16:21).

There is little doubt that Paul had a special **love for Macedonians**, as is evidenced in his letters to both the Philippians and the Thessalonians. Indeed, his letter to the Philippians simply oozes gratitude for their support of him and joy in thinking about them (e.g. Phil 1:3-5; 4:10-18). In the Thessalonian correspondence he identifies the Macedonian Christians as models in comparison to the **Achaians** (Corinthians) and those elsewhere (1 Thess 1:6-8) and he likens his relation to the Macedonians to both a nurse and a father with little children (2:7-11). It is also fascinating that in writing the Corinthians Paul indicates that nobody really wanted to visit them (1 Cor 16:7-12), that they needed to treat Timothy kindly and that perhaps he would come and stay with them for a time, but that he was definitely going to visit the Macedonians (16:5-6).

In visiting Philippi today, one cannot help but note the fact that just as the present highway bifurcates the entire site it actually follows the path of the ancient *Via Egnatia*.

South of the highway is the great agora/forum (market) with the remains of u-shaped stoa (porches) which typically opened to individual stalls that faced out on the ancient highway. In the same vicinity were several temples (which undoubtedly honored Rome and the emperor), a gymnasium (palaestra), a library, a second smaller forum and the remains of an octagonal church complex from the fifth century, part of which was built over an earlier (fourth century) Christian chapel dedicated to Paul. The complex also included a baptistery and catechetical center which employed an earlier second century BC structure dedicated to a hero by the name of Euephenes. Nearby was a earlier bath house from the first century with the typical three room pattern of the caldarium (hot), tepidarium (warm) and frigidarium (cold). Also close by was a building that has been identified as the bishop's residence. In the same vicinity are the remains of a much larger Church/Cathedral known as Basilica B which was being built in the middle of the sixth century AD but was never quite finished because the dome collapsed during construction. The foundation was not secure since it was built over an earlier theater. Much further to the south, archaeologists have discovered another large bath house with mosaic floors and both caldarium (hot) and frigidarium (cold) rooms.

[See Picture # 2 -- Traditional Site of Paul's Imprisonment]

North of the highway and up the mountain side are several important sites. The first is a cistern **traditionally** associated with the **prison** where Paul and Silas were kept when the earthquake occurred at midnight that loosened their chains (Acts 16:25-26) but it seems rather unlikely that the prison would have been in such a prominent place. Nearby are also the ruins of two other major churches. The first, often referred to as Basilica A, contained a structure which may have been a temple dedicated to the honor of Philip II. The second church from the sixth century was discovered when the local archaeological museum was being constructed. Perhaps the most significant aspect of this northern area is the **gigantic theater** of Philippi which was first

[See Picture # 3 -- The Grand Theater in Philippi]

constructed by Philip II and carved out of the side of the mountain as a grand monument to his importance. Under the Romans it was expanded several times and in my earlier article I suggested that at one time it may have seated as many as 50,000 people. During the third century the theater was modified with protective barriers to handle gladiatorial contests involving wild animals. In recent years stone masons have been working to restore the grandeur of the great theater.

Christian visitors to Philippi often request to visit the site where Paul met and baptized **Lydia** (or the Lydian woman) from Thyatira who was a seller of purple (see Acts 16:14). Several sites have been suggested such as near the Gangites River but that site which is probably at least 2 miles (3 km.) may be too far from Philippi. While it is impossible to be absolutely certain of the correct site, the one preferred by most pilgrims is the pleasant place where a **baptistry** has been constructed along the Krenides stream near the western gate of the city

[See Picture # 4 -- The Baptismal Park at Philippi]

After Paul, Philippi fades from the center of Christian discussion although **Polycarp**, the bishop of Smyrna, in the second century addressed a letter to the Christians there in order to encourage them to maintain their faith in the midst of spreading persecution.

Neapolis: **(4)** Modern Kavalla (ancient Neapolis and early medieval Christopolis) on the north shore of the Aegean Sea is today an industrial seaport and terminus for a number of ferries from the nearby Greek Islands. It is mentioned in Acts 16:11 as the bustling seaport about 10 miles (16 km.) from Philippi where **Paul first touched European soil** on his second missionary journey (c. AD 49). He undoubtedly landed here as well on his third journey and departed from here when he headed back to Jerusalem (Acts 20:1, 6).

The city was founded by settlers from the nearby island of **Thassos** between the 7th and 6th centuries BC and because the bay is protected by a half-circle of mountains and hills it forms a superb harbor. It was a member of the Athenian League during the 5th and 4th centuries BC before being conquered by Philip II of Macedon. It then passed into Roman hands in 168 BC. During the battle of 42-41 BC, which decided the fate of the Roman Republic (see Philippi), **Brutus and Cassius** anchored their ships in this bay. In the Middle Ages the city was on the frontier of the battles between the **Muslims** from Turkey (and elsewhere in the Fertile Crescent) and the Christians from Europe and it suffered several destructions, particularly in 1185 at the hands of the Norman crusaders. The Turks held this port city from 1371 until 1912 except for several periods when it came under Bulgarian domination. The picturesque aqueduct which snakes its way through the heights of the city had an initial beginning in the time of the Romans but it was fully constructed by Turkish engineers under **Suleyman the Magnificent** in the sixteenth century. The most notable citizen of the city was Mehmet Ali who was born here in 1769 and later became the Pasha of Egypt. His birthplace is open to the public. Other sites for the visitor to see include the aqueduct which is illuminated at night and the archaeological museum.

Amphipolis and Apollonia: Heading west from Philippi along the Egnaitian Highway one soon reaches the two cities of Amphipolis and Apollonia, the first being the most important.

Amphipolis: **(2)** According to Herodotus (vii. 114) the city was founded by Thracian settlers who called it "Nine Ways" (*Ennea Hodoi*) which indicated its significance as a center of commerce from various areas. After a number of attempts the **Athenians** captured the town from the Thracians in 437 BC and renamed it Amphipolis which means "around the city," a designation indicative of the fact that the Strymon River encircles much of the city. It was taken by the **Spartans** under Brasidas in 424 BC and one of the richly ornate tombs may be that of Brasidas who died in 422 defending the city during an Athenian counter assault. The city did not yield again until Phillip II conquered it in 357 BC. *Alexander G* honored it as one of his prized cities by constructing an elaborate temple there. After his death, his wife (**Roxane**) and their young son, Alexander IV, were exiled here to prevent their interference in the state affairs at Thessaloniki (Saloniki). But later they were both murdered by **Cassander**, the brother-in-law of *Alexander G* (see "Vergina" below).

The Romans took possession of it along with Philippi after the **Battle of Pydna** in 168 BC and established it as the capital of the first of four districts in Macedonia. The city prospered under Roman rule because it was both defensible and was only a short distance by river (3 miles/5 km) from the Aegean Sea, making it more convenient for access than Philippi. Still visible is a section of the old Roman wall and both a later inner and outer fortification line, It hosted many of the Roman elite and served as the naval base for **Mark Antony** in his battle with Octavian before his defeat at Actium in 31 BC.

[See Picture # 5 – The Lion of Amphipolis]

A number of significant archaeological finds have been uncovered which reflect the city's importance as one of the leading centers in Macedonia. Among them are shrines dedicated to the Phrygian god Attis and to Klio (one of the daughters of Zeus who was regarded as one of the nine muses). Also uncovered was a large gymnasium with a colonnaded palestra (exercise area) indicative of the commitment on the part of the citizens to physical development and athletic competition. Among the most well-known artifacts is the **Lion of Amphipolis** which dates to the 4th century BC and may have served as a monument honoring Leoneidon, one of Alexander's foremost admirals who confronted the mighty Persian fleet and after his outstanding service was installed as the governor of Syria. Although the Lion had been fragmented, archaeologists were able to reassemble it and today it has become the symbol of Amphipolis.

The city is mentioned in Acts 17:1 along with Apollonia as having been visited by **Paul** on his second journey after having been in Philippi (c. AD 49). During the Byzantine period it was called Popolia. In the late part of this period (5th -7th centuries) a number of large churches were constructed here, indicating that the city had a large Christian population.

Apollonia: **(a)** Just over 35 miles west of Amphipolis and along the *Via Egnatia* Luke in Acts 17:1 mentions that Paul passed the city of Apollonia which was about 33 miles east of Thessaloniki. It was a city that for all practical purposes **had faded** from history **until** some recent discoveries. When a gold wreath of ivy leaves and grapes was found by a farmer who was cultivating his field, the attention of archaeologists was immediately aroused. The reason was that the gold wreath could be dated to the middle of the 4th century BC. Further probing uncovered other artifacts, such as a statute of "Winged Victory" associated with Samothrace and a number of tombs, kilns, etc. An ancient city that had been lost since the 8th century AD had once again come to light! Moreover, archaeologists now estimate that at its height of activity during the Hellenistic period of Phillip of Macedon the city may have had a population of as many as 10,000.

Apparently the city of Apollonia became a place of refreshment that welcomed caravans and travelers on the ancient highway. Herodotus (vii. 112 ff.) notes that **Xerxes** on his military engagement against the Greeks stopped there. Others like the Apostle Paul long after him did so as well but not on his way to battle. His goal was to share the gospel.

Mount Athos: **(b)** I pause briefly to mention the most easterly of the three fingers of the Chalkidiki peninsula which lies south of Amphipolis and juts into the Aegean Sea. To the Greeks it is known as "the Holy Mountain" which houses some twenty fortified monasteries primarily from the 10th to the 16th centuries that contain some superb frescos and other artistic and literary treasures. It is a wealthy, self-governing area into which only adult males are allowed. Entrance to the enclave is highly restricted and visitors from other countries to this sanctuary mountain retreat center should obtain a letter of reference from the Greek embassy in their country of residence if they wish to enter.

Thessaloniki (Saloniki and Thessalonica): **(1)** The city was founded in 315 BC by **Cassander**, the brother-in-law of *Alexander G* and one of his **five major generals** who divided *Alexander G's* kingdom following his death in Babylon. After the vying for territories by the five settled, only three were left with kingdoms (Cassander with Macedonia and Greece, Selucus and his successors with Mesopotamia and Asia Minor, and the powerful Ptolemy [who stole the body of Alexander] with Egypt and the disputed Land of Israel).

[See Pictures # 6 a & b. -- The White Tower in Thessaloniki]
[and Mount Olympus from the White Tower]

This new city of Saloniki was located on the opposite (western) side of the Chalcidic Peninsula from Apolonia. It had a superb harbor in the northwestern corner of the Aegean Sea on the banks of the protective Thermaic Gulf, later renamed the Gulf of Salonika by Cassander for his **wife and *Alexander G's* half-sister** by Philip II. Today it is the second largest metropolis in Greece after Athens having over a million inhabitants and a major airport about 10 miles (15 km.) from the center of the city.

Strabo (Geog. vii.7) indicates that the city was built on the ruins of ancient Therma which received its name from the hot springs in the vicinity. Casander collected inhabitants from various smaller communities nearby in order to form his new city but the people refused to move to the higher defensible ground which he had chosen for the city site so during a major rain storm he had his forces **stop the drainage system** and after the subsequent flooding, the people moved to his designated location.

Thessaloniki was added to the Roman possessions in 168 BC along with the rest of Macedonia and made the capital of the second district. When Macedonia became a senatorial province in 146 BC Thessaloniki was made the **capital**. Livy (xliv. 10) reported that during the Roman-Persian war the Macedonian fleet was quartered there. When the famed orator **Cicero** became a *persona non gratia* in

Rome (c. 58 BC), he was exiled to Thessaloniki. Then in 42 BC Mark Antony and Octavian bestowed on the city colonial free status for its support in the Battle of Philippi (cf. Pliny, *Nat. hist.* iv. 36). The city continued to flourish into the 2nd century AD (cf. Lucian, *Asinus*. 46) but in the 3rd century the city had passed its prime and became engaged in battles with the Goths (AD 254). In AD 305 **Galerius**, the emperor of the eastern empire, moved his capital to Thessaloniki and the persecution of the large Christian population began in earnest.

[See Picture # 7 – The Basilica of St. Demetrius in Thessaloniki]

Among those that suffered was a Christian leader named Demetrius whose blessings were reputed to be extremely powerful. He was therefore imprisoned by Galerius in the Roman baths. The feared champion gladiator of Galerius faced off and killed a number of people in the stadium. Nestor, a blessed follower of Demetrius, was then brought up against the gladiator but in this case the champion was defeated. The death of the champion so enraged Galerius that he had Nestor killed in the stadium and also had Demetrius executed. The healing powers of the dead man thereafter continued to be reported and Demetrius was canonized. A grand basilica was erected in his honor in Thessaloniki and his icon has been said to have miraculous powers.

The city continued to resist the Muslim assaults until 905 when it was captured and burned by the Saracens. Then it suffered another devastation under the Norman crusaders in 1185. Latin and Greek Christians continually sought to unseat the others for the next two hundred years until the city fell to the Turkish Sultan Amurath II in 1430. The city was not returned to Greeks until the Balkan War of 1912 and as one might expect there followed a great deal of population upheaval and displacement after so many years of Turkish control.

The Apostle **Paul** reached the city of Thessalonica on the *Via Egnatia* from Philippi, Amphipolis and Apollonia (c. AD 49), a journey of just under 100 miles which would have taken him and his companions at least three days en route. In Thessalonica Luke indicates that Paul proclaimed the gospel in the synagogue and elsewhere, likely for a **fairly long period** (the exact length of time is probably more than merely three Sabbaths as might be assumed from Acts 17:2 since Luke was giving a thumbnail sketch of Paul's visit). The reason for this view is that in his epistles Paul states that he worked "night and day" to support himself (cf. 1 Thess 2:9; 2 Thess 3:8) and in his letter to the Philippians he notes that they sent him support several times while he was there (Phil 4:16). Soon, however, the preaching upset the local synagogue officials which led to a potential riot and caused a problem for the **city fathers**. The *free status* of the city is confirmed by the fact that the charge of "turning the world upside down" that was leveled at Jason when they could not find Paul was made before the "city fathers" (the Greek is ***politarchas***; Acts 17:6) not a Roman proconsul or tribune as in Corinth (cf. Acts 18:12). The same term is mentioned on the Varda Gate in reference to the city officials. Here, just as when Paul's preaching and evangelism caused a riot later in Ephesus (Acts 19:31), city officers who were in charge of free cities were very sensitive to anything that might disturb the *pax Romana* and bring the military into their midst.

[See Picture # 8 – A Statue of Dionysus in the Thessaloniki Museum]

The electric atmosphere caused the early Christians then to hustle Paul out of the city because he was obviously in danger. He did not dare to return immediately but by the time he wrote 1 Thessalonians, probably from Corinth, he had sent **Timothy** to check on their situation and to his relief and joy Timothy had returned and given him a good report concerning their faithfulness (1 Thess 2:17-3:10). Paul did return to Macedonia on his third journey when he took a special offering to the poor in Jerusalem where he was arrested and sent to Rome. Among those that accompanied him on his journey, Luke tells, were **Aristarchus** and Secundus from Thessalonica (Acts 20:4). We also learn that Aristarchus also accompanied Paul during his journey to Rome (Acts 27:2) and was apparently a companion prisoner of Paul during his imprisonment there (Col 4:10; Phlm 24).

Although Thessaloniki is a large city most of the important ancient sites which are on the itinerary of Christian pilgrims, as Marc Dubin's map[5] indicates, are in the town center. They include the richly carved Arch of Galerius that spanned the Via Egnatia on the east and was constructed in AD 303-04 to mark his victory over the Persians (part of the triple arch is now missing). Also in the city is the symbolic **White Tower**, an ancient fortress along the seafront which was built by the Turks in 1430 and housed prisoners. To remove the bloody stains it was painted white, thus giving rise to its name. It now serves as an historical museum. During the rebuilding process of the city after the tragic fire of August 17. 1917, the **Roman forum** of the

[See Picture # 9 - The Roman Forum in Thessaloniki]

2nd and 3rd centuries AD (earlier thought to be built over the Hellenistic agora) was uncovered lying about 6 meters (20 ft.) below street level. That fire destroyed much of the old city and severely damaged the historic church of St. Demetrius, the patron saint of the city. The crumbling historic Varda Gate which spanned the Via Egnatia at the west end of the city was unfortunately torn down 1876 and the stones were used to shore up a section of the old historic wall. The crucial **inscription** containing the description of the city fathers as *politarchas* (cf. Acts 17:6), however, was rescued and was carried to the British Museum.

Mount Olympus: (c) On a clear day looking southwest from the area of the White Tower and other parts of Thessaloniki one can see the magnificent sight of Mount Olympus (a mountain range of approximately 12 miles [20 km] in length) which is the mythical home of Zeus and the twelve Greek immortals/gods *[See Picture 6 b above.]*. Within the environs of the holy mountain is the ancient sanctuary city of **Dion.** A number of early temples from the fifth and fourth centuries BC have been uncovered but the primary significance of the sanctuary appears to have been during Hellenistic times. Philip II of Macedon celebrated his victories before Zeus here and *Alexander G* paid homage to Zeus before his departure in the conquest of his world.

Typical of the time, archaeologists have uncovered patterns of syncretistic worship where Artemis and Aphrodite have been merged with Isis. Also, uncovered are the remnants of a sanctuary to Zeus, the agora, a large theater, and evidences of athletic competitions such as a stadium and

---

[5] See Marc Dubin, consultant, *Greece: Athens and the Mainland* in Eyewitness Travel Guides (London and New York: DK, 2003), 245.

swimming pool. Also, present are evidences of the honoring of Asclepius. In addition, there are ruins of a Christian basilica from the early Byzantine period. The site suffered from a series of attacks by invaders from the north and from earthquakes. Today the area of Mount Olympus is a National Park but it is not visited on most structured tours.

Beroea/Berea (modern Veria or Ver[r]oia): (5)

In writing about the city Cicero (*In Pisonem* 36) stated that it was "a town off the beaten track." This description was a fitting evaluation of Beroea in the time of Paul who fled from Thessalonica after the potential riot there which has been recounted in Acts 17:5-9. The city lies in the hills approximately 40 miles (65km.) slightly south west of Thessaloniki, about 7 miles (12 km,) north of the royal Macedonian burial site of Vergina, and less than 25 miles (40 km.) from the historic battle site of Pydna and the Thermaic Gulf. Today it has around 50, 000 inhabitants.

It was known in earlier antiquity for its defense against the Athenians in 432 BC during the Peloponnesian War but along with the rest of Macedonia it surrendered to the Romans in 168 BC at the **Battle of Pydna** (nearby). Because it was the first to surrender to the Romans it was granted an important status in the third of the four divisions of the Macedonian Province (cf. Livy, xliv. 45; xlv. 29) but once nearby Thessalonica became the capital of the entire province, the significance of Beroea diminished rapidly. Pompey wintered his forces here in 48 BC before the battle of Pharsalos in the same year.

Luke indicates that Paul's evangelistic ministry in Beroea (c. AD 49-50) was at first very successful among both Jews and Gentiles until jealous Jews from Thessalonica arrived in the town and the Christians who were fearful for his safety immediately escorted him to the coast and on to Athens (Achaia) but Timothy and Silas remained with the believers in Macedonia (Acts 17:10-15).

[See Picture # 10 – The Memorial to Paul in Beroea]

The visitor to Beroea (Veria) today will not be welcomed to much in the way of archaeological significance in the city. I do not usually stop long with groups in this place except to show them the magnificent outdoor mosaic which depicts Paul preaching to the people and which is traditionally said to mark the *bema* or steps to the synagogue where Paul communicated the gospel. About a mile and a half north of the city archaeologists in 1960 uncovered the remains of two towers: a round one from the Hellenistic period and a square one from the period of the Gothic invasion.

By the beginning of the 4th century AD the city was prospering and **Diocletian** established the city as one of his capitals in Macedonia. During the Byzantine and Medieval periods the city continued to flourish and became the seat of a metropolitan bishopric in the late 13th century before falling to the Turks in the late 14th century. It was returned to Greek rule along with much of Macedonia in 1917.

Vergina (the ancient royal city of Aigai): (6)

While some tours of Greece by-pass this city in haste to reach Athens and the south, no visitor to Macedonia should fail to stop at the royal city of Vergina, the site of the **Macedonian Palace** (now in ruins). While the tombs of many notables were known in the area and they had been robbed by the conquering Goths and others in earlier years, the world received a startling surprise when Professor Manolis Andronikos opened the entrance to a grand Macedonian tomb in 1977 and discovered that it served as the **burial site for Philip II of Macedon**, the father of *Alexander G*. Although the treasures may not be as vast as those taken from the tomb of Tutankhamen (Tut)[6], they rank as one of the premier finds in archaeological history and the most significant discovery in Greece after Heinrich Schliemann's discovery of Mycenae[7].

The **gold casket** which contained the cremated remains of Philip II with the emblem of the sixteen point Macedonian sun/star was the adopted symbol of *Alexander G* as he conquered most of his then known world. The fact that one of the eye sockets in the skull was fractured along with other bodily impairments was adequate confirmation that it was the tomb of Philip II, the father of *Alexander G*, who had united the various city states from Macedonia to Achaea and the Peloponnese and thus formed a powerful confederacy that was able to challenge the then world power of Persia. Before his dream of world domination was fulfilled, however, Philip was assassinated in 336 BC when ***Alexander G* was 20 years of age** and his burial site had been lost until its recent discovery. The treasures of gold, silver and ivory are stunning which include items such as carved figures, crowns, wreaths, a shield and three additional tombs.

One of those tombs seems to be that of Amyntas III and a young woman who died in childbirth. It honors Persephone the so-called queen of the underworld. As the Greek myth details Pluto, the god of the underworld (the dead), was terribly lonely and came to the surface, stole the young, beautiful Persephone and carried her back to the underworld to be his queen. But the sorrow of the gods that followed resulted in the unsettling of the world (the *kosmos*) and Demeter, her mother, moved the gods to anger so that Pluto agreed to the allow Persephone to return to the surface to dance in the flowers for half of each year. This story served as the Greek mythical explanation for the seasons of the year and for the expectation that after death those who are without blame would dance in the hereafter with Persephone in the flowering meadows.

One of the **other tombs** was likely that of *Alexander G's* son, Alexander IV, who along with his mother, *Alexander G's* beautiful wife Roxane, was undoubtedly murdered in 310 BC by Cassander to secure his position in Macedonia from any infringement by his nephew.

In the vicinity are **countless other burial mounds** which have not been excavated. Although the royal palace which was expanded by Cassander (c.300 BC) into a very large complex lies in ruins, the layout provides evidence that it must have been an exceedingly impressive place. Nearby (partially excavated) is the theater where Philip II was assassinated, an act which many scholars today firmly believe was orchestrated by *Alexander G* and his mother to prevent a half- brother from assuming the throne.

---

[6] See my discussion in Gerald L. Borchert, *The Lands of the Bible*, 123, 131, 139-40.
[7] See "Mycenae" below.

In the Footsteps of Paul and John

B. CENTRAL GREECE

As one travels south through the mid section of mainland Greece, the visitor comes to some of the most unforgettable sites:

Meteora: (7) Here hermits in the 10th century AD began to live in the caves of sheer perpendicular mountain fingers that rise a thousand feet above the surrounding plain. Situated at the southern edge of the Thessalian Plain and less than 3 miles (5 km.) from the town of **Kalambaka** (population about 10,000) one arrives at the **strange cliffs** of Meteora which were formed centuries earlier by the waters of the Peneios River gushing north from the Pindos Mountains and cutting great rock crevasses in the edge of the range and leaving unusual finger-like mountain shafts as a result.

In the mid 14th century, following the conquest of the area by the Serbs and their settlement just to the south in Trikala (or Trika, the mythical home of Asclepius, the god of medicine, who learned the art of **healing from the centaur**) monks seeking to escape the distractions and temptations of population centers, retreated to these mountain hideaways and began to build their great monasteries on the tops of these unusual mountain fingers.

[See Picture # 11 -- The Union of Bones in the Grand Meteoron]

The first and largest of the monasteries to be constructed, **Megaion Meteoron** (also *Megalo Meteoro*, the "Grand Meteoron"), was founded by Athanasios Meteritis from Mt Athos on the so-called great "broad rock" (*Platys Lithos*). Climbing to it is a vigorous, time-consuming task but for the able in body it is a very rewarding experience as one can see sights like the **bone chambers** where after the flesh has disintegrated the various bones of a monk are separated and buried with colleagues who had died at a prior time. Community for them is viewed as not merely involving human life but also death as they wait together for the future life. Spending time in the **library** which houses illuminated copies of the Bible and other important religious documents and texts is a treat for those interested in seeing such rare treasures. Seeing the public rooms where the monks eat and worship is also very interesting.

[See Picture # 12 -- One of the Historic Monasteries in Meteora]

Approximately two dozen monasteries were organized in this area through the 16th century, although only about a quarter of them are still active today. *Hagia Triada* ("Holy Trinity" -1438; 1476) is a fascinating monastery; a number of the sections, such as the Chapel of St. John (*[H]Agios Ioannis*), are carved out of the stone mountain itself. *Moni Varlaam* (1518) was built on site of an earlier dwelling of hermit V(B)arlaam and the narthex of the All Saints Chapel (*Katholikon*) contains wonderful Theban frescoes. *Moni Rousanou* (1545; refounded 1639), now a convent, is perhaps the most spectacular but is not easily accessible since it was built on a very narrow needle. It contains some marvelous Cretan frescoes. The **most accessible is *Agios Stefanos* (1312), a nunnery** (but Greek does not have a name for a nunnery). It was

[See Picture # 13 – St. Stefanos Monastery in Meteroa]

commissioned by Emperor Andronikos III during his tenure (1328-41). The main church was constructed in 1798 to replace a smaller chapel and contains excellent examples of wood carvings and a finely decorated iconostasis. Like the other monasteries, it has a fascinating museum/library which is well worth the visit and the view of the Thessalian Plain from the Garden is magnificent.

Traveling south through the mountains, one reaches **Delphi**, the most sacred site in the ancient world.

[See Picture # 14 – The Ruins of the Temple of Apollo at Delphi]

Delphi (Delfi): **(8)** According to legend, **Zeus**, the supreme god in the Greek Pantheon, supposedly sent two eagles from the opposite ends of the earth and he marked the spot where they met and crossed paths in their flight. That point was the beautiful setting of Delphi which became known for Greeks as the center or **"navel" of the world**. The ancient shrine of the Delphi is situated at a height of about 1,800 ft. on the slope of Mt. Parnassos which rises to an elevation of over 8,100ft. and is located a short distance from the Bay of Itea and the Gulf of Corinth.

[See Picture # 15 – A Copy of the Navel of the World at Delphi]

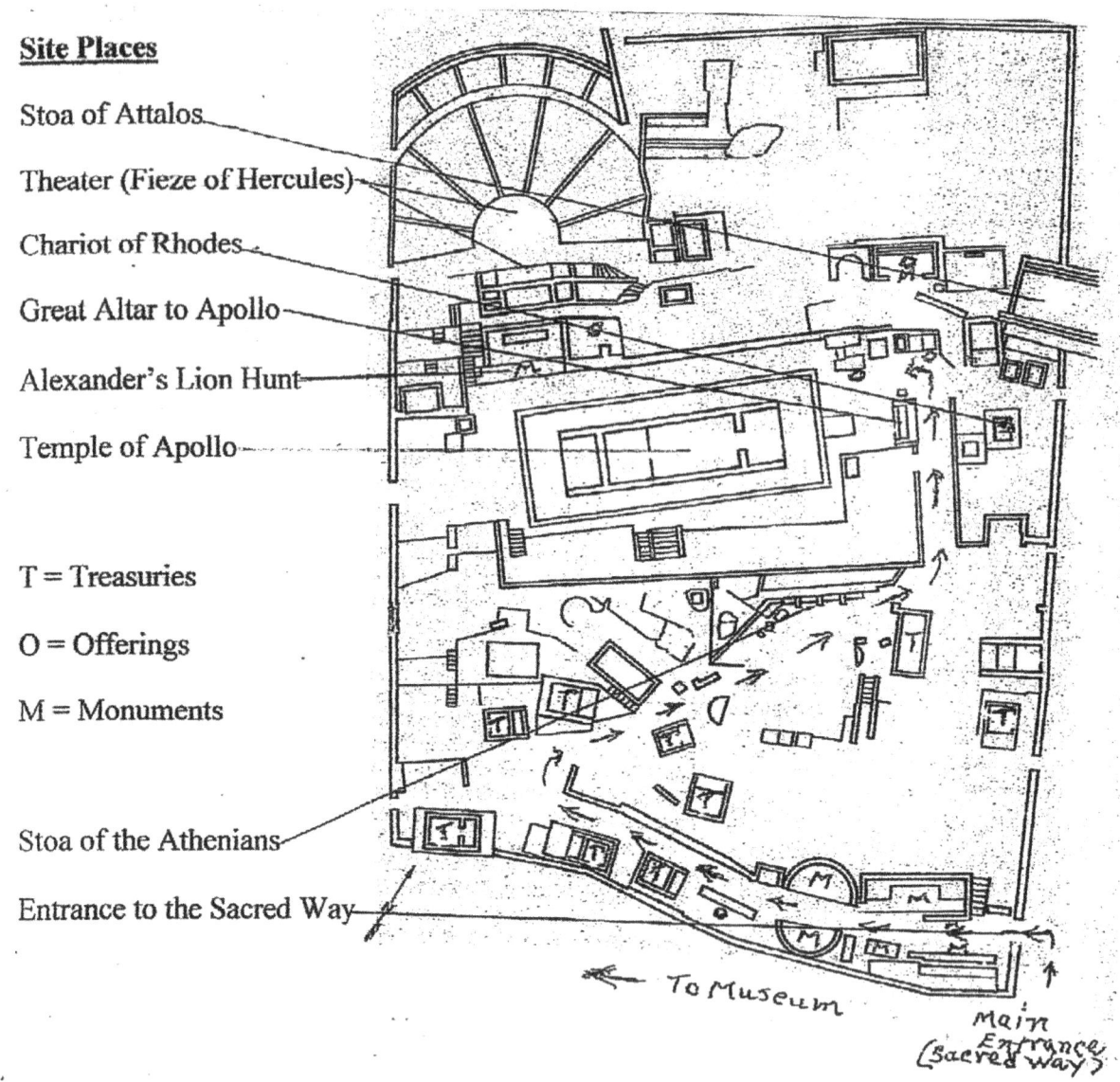

Site of Ancient Delphi

Delphi was an ancient religious center which was dedicated to the goddess Gea (Mother Earth) but, as it will become apparent, after the Dorian conquest about 1000 BC it also became associated with the god Apollo. To understand Delphi, therefore, one must recognize that the history of the **famous "Oracle"** (the place where the Greeks and many from other countries came to receive instructions/insights from the gods concerning their lives and fortunes) is encrusted with layers of myth which were synthesized in fascinating ways.

The **mythical stories** first reflect the old monster *Chronos* (time) and the willy serpent *Gea* (earth) myth in which the monster sought to gobble down the heroic child but instead was tricked into swallowing a stone. The story then becomes synthesized so that the monster somehow becomes identified with Pytho (a serpent) and the focus of worship shifts to the **Pythia priestess** who becomes the oracle for providing information concerning life, politics and the future undertakings. The story then is synthesized again with the arrival of the Dorians and their shepherd god, **Apollo**, who possessed the attributes of the sun such as light and power and was then endowed with wisdom from Pytho. To the priestess's oracular role there was then added the male priest of Apollo who became the **interpreter** of the strange ecstatic utterances of the priestess who usually was entranced by the intoxicating fumes which escaped from the earth and together the team was enabled to provide (normally the next day!) the well-known type of cryptic messages from the "divine" for the devotee who in anticipation of receiving a revelation usually had paid a handsome fee (*pelanos*) and made an animal sacrifice.

[See Picture # 16 -- The Treasury of Athens at Delphi]

By the beginning of the 7th century people were coming from almost every part of the Mediterranean world to seek the advice of the oracle. Local groups tried to control the center but during the first of the so-called religious wars (c.600-591 BC) the alliance of the Greek tribes (the Amphictyonic League) agreed that Delphi must be kept **independent, sacred and available** to all the tribes. As a result of its sanctity and its growing wealth, construction was begun (514BC) on a great Temple to Apollo (measuring 28x 195 ft.) which replaced an earlier one that had suffered from a major fire. The temple was severely damaged along with other buildings through an earthquake in 373 BC but was reconstructed in over a period of about forty years.

[See Picture # 17 -- The Picturesque Theater at Delphi]

During this same time new series of religious wars ensued which greatly affected the wealth of the center and the officers of Delphi petitioned **Philip II of Macedon** to help in settling the disputes. Philip quite willingly obliged in 338 BC and as a result united the Greek city states under his rule into a powerful confederacy which set the stage for the military exploits of his son *Alexander G.*

[See Pictures # 18 a & b -- The Charioteer and Philospher Statues in the Museum at Delphi]

The entire complex which measures roughly 620ft.x 440 ft. contains among other buildings the great **Temple of Apollo** which was the center for the oracle with the Altar of the Chians to Apollo, the Treasuries of the Athenians, the Corinthians, the Thebans, the Siphnians, the Knidians, of Potidaia, Aiolia, Kyrene, and the Archaic Treasury to give one a sense of the wealth that once poured into the center. Here was built a magnificent 4th century Theater which seated 5,000 people which provided the spectators with an incredible view that overlooked the entire mountain valley. Also in the complex are the Boleuterion (council chamber), the Meeting Hall of the Knidians and several Stoa (porches). Even walking through the complex today, much of which lies in ruins, gives one sense of the **incredible wealth** that must have poured into the center. Visitors to Delphi will not want to miss the remarkable little museum which contains many fine marble sculptured items and ornate decorations including the famous bronze statue of the charioteer and the Sphinx of the Naxians. Also included in the museum are items which are reminders of the serious earthquake that damaged Delphi. High above the complex the ancients built a great Stadium/Hippodrome for horse and chariot racing. The climb rewards visitors with an excellent example of seeing the fine remains of a classic structure.

[See Picture # 19 – The Stadum/Hippodrome in Delphi]

Below the complex was a 4th century stadium which would seat approximately 7000 and was built over an earlier one from the 5th century which was used for the Pythian games. Nearby was a grand sports complex (gymnasium) with baths, massage rooms, a running track and a wrestling center; everything to encourage fitness. The **Romans** entered the picture in 191 BC and later enhanced the entire stadium area with a Triumphal Arch. The Goths made an effort to conquer the shrine in 109 BC but were repulsed. In the following years, however, many of the treasures of Delphi were carried off to Rome, especially by Nero who was searching for funds to rebuild the city. Although the shrine in the succeeding generations lost much of it appeal, it was not finally closed until **Theodosius** declared its termination as a religious site in AD 381.

Among the most important treasures for biblical scholars is the fragmentary inscription in the museum of Delphi which refers to Gallio as the Proconsul of Achaia. The inscription is strategic because it enables us to date the presence of Gallio in Achaia and since Proconsuls were generally appointed by the Roman Senate for a maximum of one or two years it enables us to establish the presence of Paul at Corinth at around AD 52 (See Acts 18:12).

[See Picture # 20 – Inscription Concerning Gallio at Corinth in the Delphi Museum]

C. ATHENS AND THE IMMEDIATE AREA OF ATTICA:

(9, 20) To write a brief introduction to Athens is an almost impossible task. It has been called the cradle of western civilization even though some may dispute the designation and attribute such a title to Mycenae or some other settling. But whatever one might say, Athens (the heart of the area called Attica) is one of the most significant cities in the history of the world.

[See Picture # 21 – The Acropolis of Athens at Night]

A Brief Historical Review: The early history of Athens like that of Delphi is **encrusted with myth** which may stretch back to 5000 BC but we are aware from some archaeological remains that there was a small village in the area as early as 3500 BC. In approximately 2000 BC the Ionians (also known as Hellens) migrated to Attica and they had a king by the name of **Kekrops** who is reputed to have had the head of a man but the body of a snake. Some of the following rulers were seemingly god-men types who apparently were descended from Athena and likewise had a serpentine body. Then according to Homer (Odyssey vii. 81-82) about the late 14th century BC **Erechtheus** fortified the hill which has become known as the acropolis. Later **King Aigeus** (after whom Aegean Sea is named) sent his son **Theseus** to Crete to kill the Minotaur (the evil god with the head of a bull) who had been demanding sacrifices of young Athenians (See also the discussion concerning **Heraklion, Crete**). The king had given instructions that when they returned dark sails should not be used unless the mission failed. But although Theseus killed the Minotaur, he forgot to hoist the white sails as he returned and Aigeus thinking that the Athenians were doomed committed suicide by throwing himself off the Acropolis. The story was basically told to celebrate the amazing deeds of Theseus who (like Samson in the Bible) was known for his remarkable feats of bravery.

When one proceeds to the period from the 10th to the 7th centuries BC, Athens became known for its artistry in terms of sculpture, pottery and painting and items such as its vases which have been found throughout the Mediterranean basin. During this time the authority of the king was greatly reduced and the political strength of the nobility rose so that by the early 7th century real power vested in the **archons** (usually nine in number) who lived in and controlled the Agora as well as all the various areas of city politics. During this time the lower classes suffered greatly under the ruthlessness of these rich rulers/tyrants.

By the beginning of the 6th century **Solon** emerged to champion the **rights of the underprivileged** and reformulated the laws to bring honesty to business practices, eliminate servitude for indebtedness, produce fairness in taxation practices, in addition to leading Athens to become an international power (Does it sound like a familiar dream, even today?) One of his major achievements was the development of a council of four hundred to offset the historic power of the elite in the **Areopagus** (note Acts 17:22). Unfortunately, the reforms of Solon did not last long but the seed had been sown for a new system of government that would not die easily. He was followed by Peisistratos (546-528 BC) an absolute authoritarian but at least he was not as harsh on the lower class as the archons had been. During his time drama and literature were greatly encouraged. His sons, however, who followed their father were exceedingly harsh. In 510 BC the Delphic Oracle solemnly declared that the **Acropolis** was sacrosanct and forbad any future dwelling by mortals on the Holy Mountain.

[See Pictures # 22 – The Acropolis from the Odeon of Herodes Atticus & # 23 – The Theater of Dionysus from the Acropolis]

In 507 BC a new reformer emerged in **Kleisthenes** who developed the system of dividing the various areas of Attica into separate sections and a council of 500 was elected by an early kind of ballot or lot. He also maintained the role of the archons but in this case they were also elected. The strength of Athens soon began to return and by 499 it challenged the power of Persia which had expanded to the islands of the Aegean. The Persian king **Darius** then responded by attacking the Greek mainland in nearby Marathon (490) although the Greeks were able to gain the victory. About ten years later **Xerxes**, his son, tried again but also failed. Even though Athens and Piraeus (its seaport) had suffered in the battles, the task of rebuilding was begun in earnest. Among the heroes in the battles with the Persians were Themistocles and Kimon but while they were excellent warriors, they did not fit the Athenian mind-set for adequate politicians and each of them suffered exile not long after their victories.

[See Picture # 24 – The Asclepion from the Acropolis]

The stage was thus set for the coming of **Pericles** (Perikles) and the **"Golden Age of Athens."** In 462 BC he moved north and emerged in Athens as its leader in the struggle against Sparta. During his tenure philosophy, science and the arts all flourished and the names of people like Socrates, Sophocles and Herodotus became legends to which one could add scores of others such as architects like Mnesicles and Kallicrates, as well as sculptors like Pheidas and Myron. Also, during his time great building projects were initiated such as the rebuilding of the Propylaea (grand entrance) and the Parthenon on the Acropolis in addition to the new Temples of Dionysus and Hephaistus, the Odeion of Pericles and the Gymnasium of Lycion. Pericles died in 429 just after the outbreak of the second **Peloponnesian War** which greatly weakened Athens in its leadership among the Greeks. As a result, a new series of battles was initiated by **Sparta** which ultimately led to its emergence as the leader of the Greeks. Nevertheless, Athens continued to develop its cultural leadership through persons like Plato and Aristophanes and its building program expanded with the construction of structures like the **Erecthion** (Erechtheion), the double temple to both Athena and Poseidon which honored its 14th century king on the acropolis as well as shrines to Hygeia and Asclepius below.

The 4th century was a period of political unrest in Athens although **philosophy, rhetoric and the arts** continued in their ascendancy with notables such as Aristotle, Isocrates, Demosthenes as well as the sculptural school of Kephisodotos and a number of other artisans and artists. During this time Lykougos erected the magnificent theater of Dionysus below the acropolis and the stadium. But the bell of power was tolling for Athens with the emerging of Macedonian power. In August 338 BC on the plain of Chaironeia about 90 miles (145 km.) north of Athens the Macedonians under **Philip II and his son Alexander** won a decisive victory over the combined forces of Athens and Thebes (Thivai).

After a series of defeats in the 3rd century, one at the hands of **Pergamum** (vassals of Rome), the Romans took a clear interest in the welfare of Athens. Finally in 168 BC at the battle of Pydna the Macedonians were soundly defeated and Athens was treated as free and independent city. But Athens fell under the domination of **Pontus** and even supported Pontus in its fight against Rome. The reaction was that **Sulla** sacked Athens in 86 BC. But Rome did not continue in its negative attitude to Athens because of Rome's great admiration for the culture of Athens, both supporting and encouraging its rebuilding. By 27 BC its free city status was restored by **Augustus** who added to the city's prestige by constructing a Roman forum in the city and a temple on the acropolis. Nevertheless, during this period Athens had **shrunk** in size to around 25,000 even though its cultural influence far surpassed almost any other city in the Roman Empire.

Paul probably reached Athens either by land or by sea (c.49-50) from Beroea (we cannot be sure, although Acts 17:14 may suggest it was by sea). Moreover, even though his visit to Athens was brief, he nevertheless delivered his very important **Areopagus address** employing arguments from natural theology which Luke summarizes in a full twenty verses (15-34) in Acts 17. The reason Paul apparently spent little more time in Athens was because the population center of the region was Corinth. We are aware of no letters he addressed to the Athenians even though he apparently had gained some converts there, including a council member named Dionysius (17:34). We also know that the Stoics and Epicureans who are mentioned in 17:18 had almost opposing philosophical perspectives on life and so we can surmise that Paul was engaged in a lively debate with them. Moreover, we also know that these philosophers would spend their time in porches or *stoa* (the name from which **"Stoic"** is derived) of the *agora* (market) seeking to convince people of their views. The **concept of the resurrection** would have been very foreign to them because they believed in the immortality of the soul. Accordingly, some scholars have suggested that Paul's use of natural revelation in his argument with the philosophers in verses 26-29 was a failure but such is not the conclusion which Luke suggests to the story. Finally, we know that Paul was ready to use any legitimate type of argument as long as it pointed to Christ (cf.1Cor 9:21-23) in order to convince people of their need for salvation. This story is thus a model for us of how to reach people with whom we have little previous connection.

[Picture # 25 – The Areopagus (Mars Hill) from the Acropolis]

In the years following the time of Paul, Athens continued to attract the elite thinkers of Rome and elsewhere in the Empire, including **Hadrian** who was one of the most able and astute emperors and who favored Athens, even erecting in it a gate in his honor (AD 131) and dedicating the great **Temple to Olympian Zeus** during the Panhellenic Festival the next year. This magnificent temple, which was constructed on the flat plain just beyond the Acropolis area, measured 315 feet (96 m.) x 130 feet (40 m) with 104 Corinthian columns (15 still stand) and was the largest in all of Greece, even surpassing the Temple of Athena in size but not in grandeur.

Then in the succeeding centuries Athens suffered from a series of misfortunes: attacks from foreign enemies, its artistic treasures were **looted** by the emperors to enhance the new capital of Constantinople, a devastating earthquake, and disputes over and termination of the Olympic Games. With the **Christianizing of Greece**, many of the temples were either closed or transformed into churches and by the 9th century even the Parthenon was transformed into a cathedral. Athens also became embroiled in the disputes between the eastern and western churches and since it was aligned with Constantinople over against the Roman Church it suffered attacks from the west during the 12th through the 14th centuries. In 1546 it was captured by **Mehemed II** and the Turkish Muslims who held it until the 19th century. During the Turkish period the Acropolis suffered **two serious blows** when gunpowder was stored up there: lightning struck the Propylaia and severely damaged it in 1645 and in 1687, during the Venetian attack, the center of Parthenon was ripped apart by a stray canon missal hitting the ammunition storage.

In the Footsteps of Paul and John

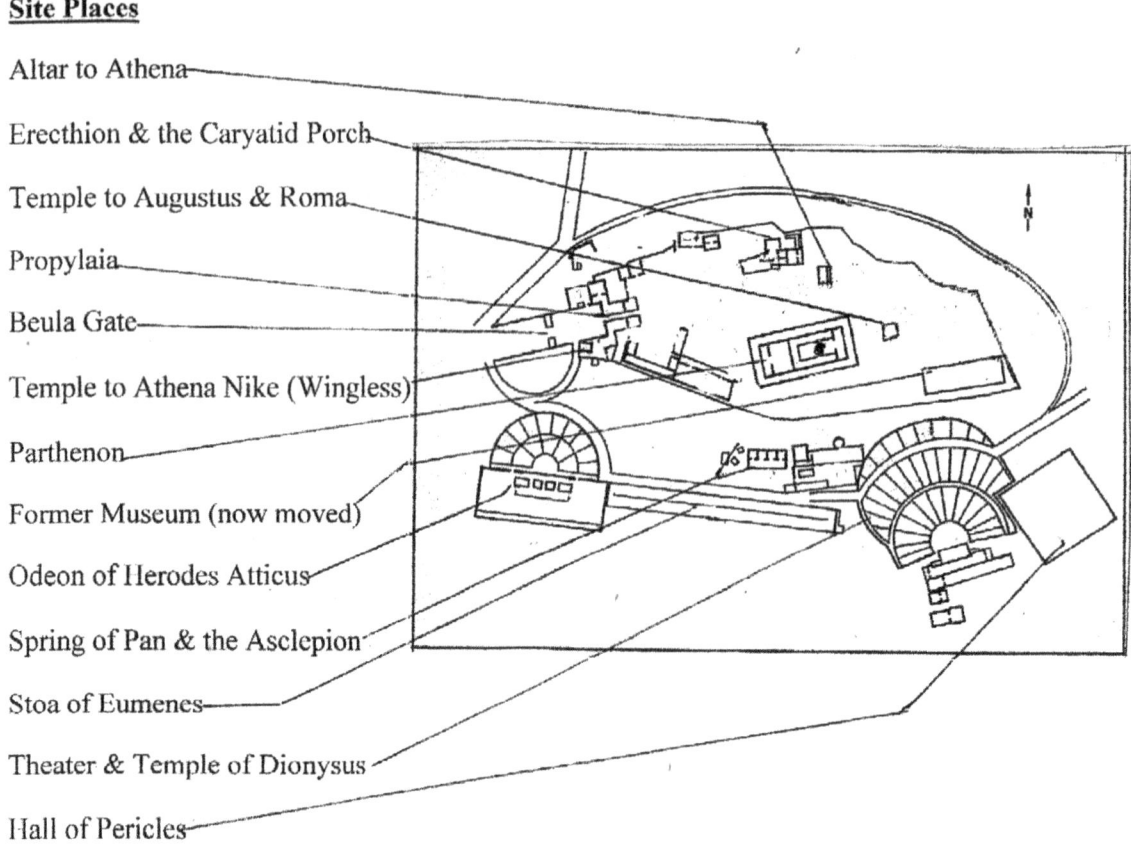

Site Places
- Altar to Athena
- Erecthion & the Caryatid Porch
- Temple to Augustus & Roma
- Propylaia
- Beula Gate
- Temple to Athena Nike (Wingless)
- Parthenon
- Former Museum (now moved)
- Odeon of Herodes Atticus
- Spring of Pan & the Asclepion
- Stoa of Eumenes
- Theater & Temple of Dionysus
- Hall of Pericles

Site of the Athenian Acropolis

The Bravarians under Ortho "liberated" Athens and set up the Kingdom of Greece in 1833 after a Greek revolution and a series of battles. But the city has since that time seen many periods of conquest and unrest although it has continued to grow from a very small town of a few thousand to a metropolis today of over three million.

Visiting Athens today: The city of Athens contains many treasures for the visitor to see but it is wise not to attempt a tour in a day as some companies seek to do. If, however, one is rushed, fortunately many of most significant monuments are in the fairly confined area of the Acropolis.

Climbing the monumental steps to the **Acropolis** which rises over 500 ft. above the plain is an effort for some people but it is a breathtaking experience. While ascending the monumental steps, on the right one sees the small Temple to ***Nike*** ("Victory") but the Athenians designated her as "wingless" *Nike* because after the victorious sea battle with the Persians they clipped her wings so that she would not leave Athens. Moving forward, one passes through the **Propylaia**, the great entrance hall, which had been rebuilt several times but the one that was constructed in 437 BC was an architectural marble prize with five magnificent doorways, the central one serving for religious processions which involved bringing in animals to be sacrificed to the gods. The inside of the structure was like an elaborate waiting room where people could rest after the climb and Pausanius (I. xxii. 5ff.) indicates it was like a great art gallery. Unfortunately, these treasures were **looted** during conquests and the building itself suffered severe damage from various, earthquakes, wars and from the explosion of munitions that were stored there during the Turkish period.

[See Picture # 26 – The Sacrosanct Double Temple (Erecthion) Dedicated to both Poseidon and Athena with the Celebrated Caryatid Porch]

Upon reaching the top of the Acropolis (measuring c. 900 x 500 ft.) one sees the remains of two great ancient structures. The one ancient structure is the marble **Erecthion** (built at the end of the 5th century BC) which was named for the mythical king Erectheus in Homer (see above) and in fact it became the most sacrosanct building on the Acropolis. While Athens traditionally honored Athena, after the great naval battle with the Persians, the Athenians were faced with divided loyalties. But naturally there is a myth associated with the building of this sacred shrine. The myth involves a test between Athena and Poseidon. Both gods vied for recognition by the Athenians and to seek the devotion of the people Poseidon struck the rock on the acropolis with his trident and the creature that emerged frightened the devotees. But when Athena struck the rock, out grew an olive tree, the symbol for the Athenians of peace. The decision was clear. The Athenians chose Athena but to avoid angering Poseidon the wise Athenians built a double temple to **Poseidon and Athena** and a legend arose to support their decision. On the south side, to provide finished form for the double temple a special porch was constructed as the tomb for the mythical King **Kekrops** who had the body of a snake (see above) with beautiful **Caryatid-like pillars** (carved women carrying containers on their heads). During the Turkish period the Erecthion was used by the Turkish commanders for various purposes, including the residence for his harem (1463). In 1801 Lord Elgin removed one of Caryatids from the porch and took it to Britain. The building was almost destroyed in 1827 by a Turkish shell during the war of independence.

[See Pictures # 27 – Some Original Caryatid Columns in the Acropolis Museum & # 28 – The Caryatid Porch of the Erecthion]

The other great structure on the Acropolis is the magnificent 230 x 100 ft. (70 x 30 m.) **"Temple" to Athena** (the **Parthenon**) designed by Kallicrates where the huge 40 ft. (12 m.) ivory and gold statue of the goddess used to stand holding her spear with the golden point which sailors could allegedly see for miles out to sea and which served as a guide for their ships. This treasury is one of those ancient wonders of construction in which the architect planned to compensate for the curvature of the eye by setting the pillars tilted slightly inward and the corner pillars set slightly out so that the entire temple appears to be at right angles and the rectangles are designed on the 9 to 4 ratio to give the appearance of beauty and harmony, two of the great virtues of Greek philosophy. Architects still study the Parthenon as a model of an ideal structure.

[See Pictures # 29 – Frieze from the Parthenon in the Acropolis Museum & # 30 – The Front of the Parthenon]

In the Footsteps of Paul and John

One of the great controversies concerning the acropolis is the activity of **Lord Elgin** who was stationed in the Mediterranean area at the beginning of the 19th century. In 1801-03 he successfully negotiated with the Turks to remove the marble friezes (also called the Elgin marbles) from the Parthenon and sold them to the British government who deposited them in the British Museum for the purposes of preservation. As already indicated, he also had one of the Caryatid pillars removed from the Erectheion as well as friezes from the Temple of Nike during the same period

An aftermath of the many wars that have ravaged Athens is that the Acropolis has a great deal of stone rubble. In 1878 (reconstructed after World War II) a small museum was erected on the site that once was the Ergasterion (the Temple built to honor both Rome and Augustus) which was in ruins and which the Greeks did not intend to reconstruct. More recently, however, a new magnificent **Acropolis Museum** has been constructed a short distance from the Acropolis. Here are displayed many of the damaged stone pieces that have been rescued. Here also are now housed the original Caryatid pillars in order to preserve them and copies have been inserted instead in the Erectheion. Today visitors to the Acropolis will often see stone masons at work with restoration projects, particularly on the Parthenon.

Below the Acropolis on the south side are the great **Theater of Dionysus**, the son of Zeus, which after its major phase of construction under to supervision of Lykourgos (c.330 BC) seated 17,000 witnessed plays from all the Greek writers including: Sophocles and Euripides. During the Christian and Turkish periods many of the faces of the gods in friezes and statues have been removed or destroyed as a desecration of the pagan worship. Behind the theater near the acropolis hill is a chapel cave (Panagia Spilliotissa containing the sacred spring of Pan). The cave was used from various purposes including the divine processional before the plays began. To the west of that theater is the **Odeon of Herodes Atticus** which was built in AD161 (restored in 1955) and is used regularly today for outdoor performances and concerts. Between these two major structures was the long Stoa (porch) of Eumenes and behind it was the shrine dedicated to Asclepius who was originally a water god and became the dispenser of rest, relaxation and healing. Recalling that the ancient plays often lasted up to 8 hours should provide a key to the interrelationship of these structures.

Just west, slightly to the north and below the entrance to the Acropolis is located the **Areopagus** (sometimes called Mars Hill), the once supreme council of the Athenians where Paul delivered his famous address (see Acts 17). Nothing now exists on this hill and earlier it was difficult for some people to climb but now the authorities have constructed a wide metal staircase that makes the ascent very easy. From this point one is able to gain an excellent view of the large ancient Greek Agora (market).

From this vantage point as one looks down on the Agora (the Main Market), one notices the best preserved white columned temple in the area which is the **Temple of Hephaistos,** the god of fire, (c. 450-440 BC) that even retains the roof in fairly good condition. Many Greeks refer to it as the Temple to Thesius (**Thesion**), the Greek heroic king who is honored in mythology for killing the Minotaur. Many of the sculptural decorations relate to the feats of Hercules and Theseus which undoubtedly gave rise to its confusing identification.

[See Picture # 31 – The Temple of Hephaistos (also known as the Thesion)]

Immediately behind it originally was the general council chamber of the city (Bouleuterion). To the right near the Acropolis there once stood the south stoa and in front of it there were two small temples and a middle stoa with a series of statues facing the center of the Agora and the Temple of Ares. At the far end stands the **reconstructed Stoa of Attalus** which was originally built by King Attalus II of Pergamum (159-38 BC) when he functioned as a caretaker of Athens on behalf of Rome. American archaeologists rebuilt the stoa using much of the material they were able to salvage during their diggings and once it was completed the stoa was established as the museum repository for the exhibits that were discovered in the Agora. In front of the Stoa of Attalus once stood the **Bema** which could serve as a place for the delivery of orations or for the declaration of judgments.

[See picture # 32 – The Stoa of Attalus in the Agora (Reconstructed)]

Beyond the immediate area of the Acropolis and a short distance to the east of the Theater of Dionysus lies the Roman Forum/Agora (market) and the great Temple of Olympian Zeus (the Roman Jupiter). To the north of the Acropolis is the **National Archaeological Museum** which is one of the finest in the world and includes the discoveries of Heinrich Schliemann who uncovered Mycenae (see below) and its golden treasures such as the so-called death mask of Agamemnon. In this museum are also artifacts from the volcanic island of Santorini (ancient Thira) which is on the itinerary of many tours to the Greek Islands (see below). Besides a great collection of Greek statues and bronze items (such as the horse and the little Jockey) there is also a magnificent display of pottery as well as some fascinating treasures which were raised from ships that were sunk during sea battles of the past. Reflecting on my first visit to Athens, I remember vividly spending a day in this magnificent museum and I have since returned a number of times to consider these memorials from the ancients.

[See Pictures # 33a, b & c. – Gold Death Masks, The Little Jockey &Aphrodite being Tempted by Pan and Eros & #34. – A Bronze Statue of Agustus, the Pontifix Maximus (12 BC). All are in the National Archaeological Museum in Athens]

D. THE CITIES OF THE PELOPONNESE

According to the Greek myth or legend associated with Olympia (See below), Pelops, the local ruler of the nearby town of Pisa won the hand of Hippodemeia, the daughter of Oinomaos, the king of Olympia, by beating him in a chariot race. The chariot races at Olympia were therefore initiated, as the story goes, to remember this historic race. Moreover, because of this strategic victory, the myth asserts that the entire area became know as the *Peloponnesos* (Pelop's Island), even though the Peloponnese is not actually an island.

A narrow isthmus separates the Greek mainland from the southern region known as the Peloponnese and the city of Corinth virtually sits on the isthmus. Ships sailing between the east

(Ephesus and Asia Minor) and the west (Rome and Italy) sought to avoid the underwater rocks around the horn of Greece (see Strabo, *Geog.* viii. 8.20) which because of the dangers the area became known to the ancients as the home of the mythical **Sirens** (nymphs who lured sailors into their abode by singing). Since many ships were lost around the horn (Cape Maleae) and the voyage took nearly two weeks, several emperors including Julius Caesar had dreamed of cutting a canal across the land bridge. **Nero** actually began the process in AD 67 but failed in the task because of the hardness of the rock and the sheer depth of the rock face at that point. His goal was to avoid dragging the smaller ships on a moveable platform (***diolkos*** from which we get the word dolly) across the narrow isthmus of less than 4 miles (6 km.) or paying stevedores to unload larger ships at the port of **(10) Cenchreae** (to the east on the Saronic Gulf and the Aegean Sea) transport the cargo overland and reload it on other ships at the port of **(10) Lechaion** (Lechaeum, to the west on the Gulf of Corinth and the Adriatic Sea). The Corinthian canal was not finished until the 19th century when gunpowder was used to accomplish the task. To stand at the top of the canal and look down gives an immediate perception of the reason why the task was not completed earlier.

[See Picture # 35 – The Corinthian Canal]

Corinth: **(10)** I have often asked my students: What are currants? The answer is: the British term for raisins which are in fact dried grapes. But beyond that fact, currant is a defective form of Corinth which hints at the fact that among the major products shipped from Corinth were grapes and wine. But the name Corinth is probably derived from Corinthus who was a supposed son of Zeus. Because of the strategic position of Corinth between the east and west of the Mediterranean basin and the north and south of Greece, by the time of Paul it had become a very **cosmopolitan city** but it had been in existence for a very long time as a Greek village and city prior to that period.

Several Myths are associated with Corinth and according to one it was said that Corinth was founded by the deceptive Sisyphus, according to Homer and others, and even though he managed to escape "Death," he was ultimately captured by Hermes, sent to Hades and was punished by being required to roll a heavy stone up a hill continually. The theme of these myths emphasizes the deceptiveness and craftiness of the Corinthians who became wealthy sea-faring merchants throughout the Mediterranean basin. Among the many gods worshipped by the Corinthians, seven Doric columns remain of a magnificent sixth century Temple to Apollo, the traveling Sun god, who was clearly honored here.

[See Picture # 36 – The Temple of Apollo in Corinth]

Its history goes back to the Late Stone Age (Neolithic period) and it was no doubt influenced by the Mycenaeans and it was constantly besieged by outsiders. Its inhabitants basically fought to survive. In its more recent history (c. 1000 BC) Dorian immigrants from the north settled in the area near an earlier, small Phoenician village and they developed the harbors which were named (see above) after the supposed sons of Poseidon. Trade rapidly developed following the rise of the **Baccaid** dynasty (747 BC) and Corinth founded colonies in several Mediterranean ports such as at Corfu and Syracuse. The Baccaids were succeeded by the tyrant Cypselus (657 BC) until his son, the renowned **Periande**r gained the throne (627) and ruled for forty years. The golden years of wealth and building in Corinth followed and like many after him Periander contemplated the building of a great canal for shipping goods from east to west and making Corinth the center of the Mediterranean world. But failing that vision, he built a grooved road that facilitated moving dollies (*diolkos*) that carried smaller vessels across the isthmus.

Among the products exported from there over the centuries were not only agricultural goods but **Corinthian bronze** became one of the most highly desired decorations in the ancient world and it was even used later on the great door of the new Jewish Temple (Josephus, *War*, v. 200-205). During this period Corinthian architecture and pottery also became prized throughout the Mediterranean world. The Corinthians soon realized the need for a navy to support their trading ships and they developed the fast moving attack vessel known as the trireme which had three banks of oars.

But being situated between Athens and Sparta and in the middle of their **constant battles** soon had a choking effect on Corinth. Although Corinth survived both the Peloponnesian Wars (431-04 BC) and the subsequent Corinthian War (395-87), it was not a dominant power until **Phillip II** of Macedon moved into the region and chose Corinth to be his **capital** for the southern Hellenic League (338 BC). Then in 196 BC Rome came on the scene and allowed the southern Greek cities some sense of independence and Corinth became the head of the so-called Achaean League. But the Greeks soon wanted their independence: Sparta spurned Corinthian dominance and the Corinthians purposely disgraced the Roman envoys. The gauntlet had been thrown down and Rome answered with force. **Lucius Mummius** soundly defeated the Greeks in 146 BC then sacked and burned Corinth, much like the north burned Atlanta in the American Civil War.

From that time, it lay mostly in ruins for a hundred years until **Julius Caesar** decided that the area was prime real estate and that the city was once again needed. So, in 46 BC he ordered it to be rebuilt, designated it as a Roman colony (*Colonia Laus Julia Corinthiensis*) and populated it with both Italians and Greeks, both free and slaves. And like Atlanta, it rose again from the ashes to become a **great new city** that attracted people from many lands. The Romans joined sections of the mainland to the Peloponnese in order to form the new province of Achaia and the Roman Senate conferred on the area the designation of a **"Senatorial Province"** in which Corinth became the actual capital (no longer Athens) with a senior Roman Senator like **Gallio** (see Acts 18:12) serving as its proconsul (See Picture # 20 for the **inscription** concerning the presence of the Proconsul Gallio in Achaia which is housed in the Delphi Museum).

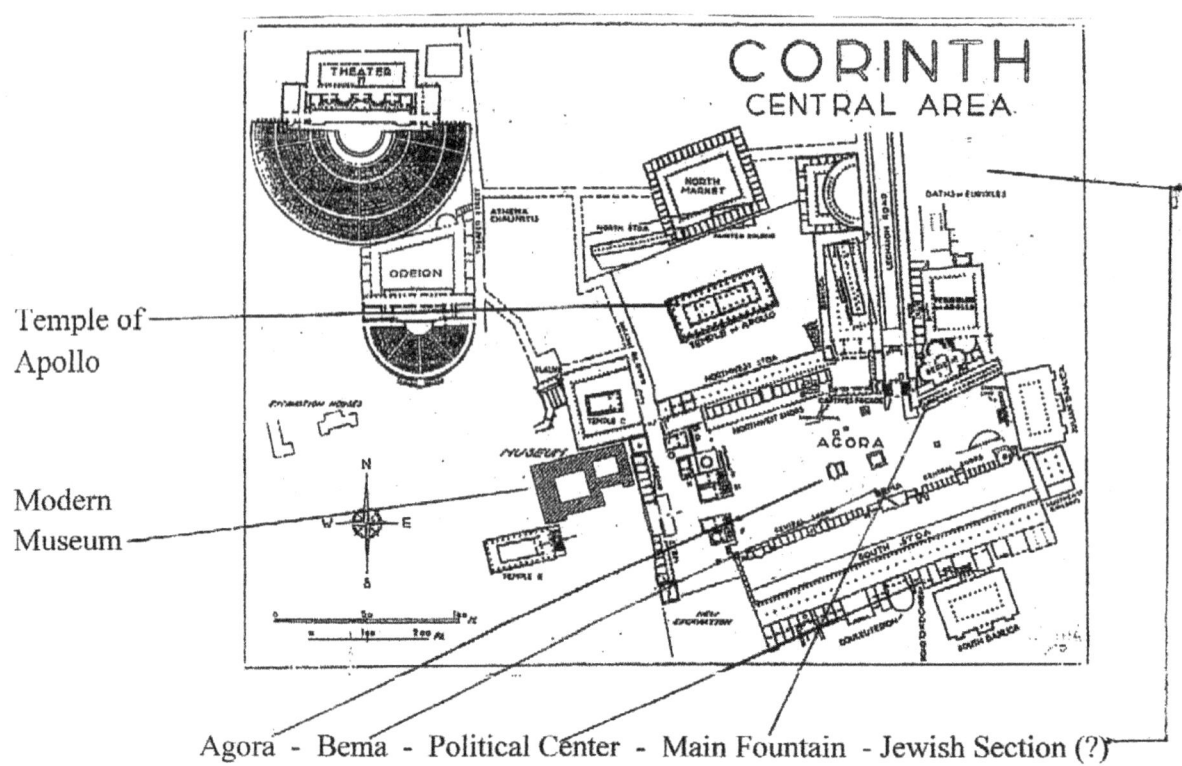

Site map of Corinth

To say that Corinth became Roman is an understatement and succeeding emperors gave it a favored status. By the time of Paul, many of the people were very affluent, very proud of their status, very cosmopolitan and the city attracted religious views of every sort. Because it was a seaport it also had a reputation that one could find many varieties of entertainment and loose living there. Strabo (*Geog.* viii. 20) also argued that the **Temple of Aphrodite on the Acrocorinth** had a thousand prostitute priestesses serving there. That statement has been repeated countless times in churches and elsewhere but while the city and temple did provide such service, other research suggests that the statement is highly exaggerated because Strabo's purpose was to shock his readers. Nevertheless, one could easily add that Corinth was not a city for everyone and certainly one has the sense from Paul in 1 Corinthians 16 that none of the Christian missionaries were very anxious to visit or revisit the city. Accordingly, one might reflect further on another of **Strabo's statements**: "Not for every man is the voyage to Corinth."[8]

When **Paul** left Athens and arrived in Corinth, he met with two Jews who had been banished from Rome (Aquilla and Priscilla) and stayed with them. That note would coordinate with the Edict of Claudius in **AD 49** which banished Jews from Rome. Paul followed his practice of visiting the

---

[8] See Strabo, *Geog.* viii. 378. *Ou pantos andros es Korinthon esth ho plous.* For other references see Hans Conzelmann, *1 Corinthians* in Hermeneia (Philadelphia: Fortress Press, 1975), 12.

Jewish synagogue and proclaiming the gospel (cf. Acts 18:1-4). Here he seems to have been fairly successful during this period of about a year and a half because even **Crispus**, the leader of the synagogue, believed along with others including Gentiles. But Paul's success angered the Jews and they initiated a charge against him of violating Roman law with the Proconsul **Gallio**. Paul was thereupon hauled before Gallio's Bema.

[See Picture # 37 a & b. – The Bema where Paul Appeared before Gallio in the Agora at Corinth and the Arocorinth with the Historic Temple of Aphropdite on the top in the Background]

But instead of accepting the Jewish charge Gallio condemned the Jews for instigating unrest (or breaking the Roman peace) and he had them punished. Among them was Sosthenes who appears to have become the new leader of the synagogue (cf. Acts 1812-17). It is intriguing to speculate on whether this **Sosthenes** was the same person as the one listed in 1 Corinthians 1:1 who was a follower of Jesus.

[See Picture # 38 – An Inscription from the Ancient Jewish Synagogue in Corinth]

When one reads the Corinthian correspondence, however, it becomes quite clear that the Apostle Paul had his hands full with the Corinthians. He had a number of encounters with them as suggested in his letters. Indeed, it is likely that he wrote more than two letters to them which are lost. For instance he indicated in one (1 Cor. 5:9) that he had already written not to associate with immoral people and in another (2 Cor. 2:4) that he wrote a painful letter to them. There has been considerable speculation concerning these remarks. But what can be said is that the letters we do have from Paul fortunately provide a great deal of insight into the lives of Corinthian Christians and they offer important perspectives to us concerning **integrity** in Christian living.

Although Corinth today is in ruins, visitors to the ancient city can stand in agora like Paul before **Bema** (the seat of authority) where Gallio pronounced his judgment. On the north they can walk through the remains of the elevated (Archaic) Temple of Apollo with seven of its thirty-eight large pillars still standing and visit the north Agora, they can walk over to the Lechaion Road and gaze up at the Acrocorinth that rises to a height of 1886 ft. (570 m.) where the historic Temple of Aphrodite stood or if they have at least three hours they can climb the mountain and view the entire landscape before returning to the plain below. They can then reenter the Forum area pass the front line of shops and the Julian Basilica to see what were the official offices including the council chambers before heading west to the Temple of Hera and both the Odeon and the Theater. There are other sites but a visit to the small museum here is also important. In it you will see items from Mycenaean period, the heads of Nero and Tyche and in the courtyard a 4th century inscription reading "Synagogue of the Hebrews." If the curator or the officer in charge will open the area, the **Asclepeion Room** is fascinating because it contains clay replicas of body parts and other items which give us a fairly adequate picture of their understanding of medicine at the time.

[See Picture # 39 – Replicas of Body Parts Recovered from the Asclepion in Corinth]

After leaving Corinth, most tours from Athens appropriately also visit at least Mycenae and Epidaurus. Therefore, they are included here.

Mycenae (also Mykine/Mycene):

(11) Following the decline of the Minoan culture, Mycenae emerged as a strong successor. Although there seems to have been sporadic occupation at the site since the 7th millennium BC, it was not until near the beginning of the 2nd millennium BC (the Middle/Late Bronze Age) that the city of Mycenae emerged as significant. Legend suggests that the city was founded by **Perseus**, the son of Zeus and that he constructed the citadel (fortified palace complex) and the main wall with the help of the **Cyclopes** (thus the name, the "Cyclopean Wall") which in sections was as much as 46 ft. (14 m.) wide. The triangular city was protected by steep cliffs which at places reached more than 160 ft high. As the city grew, the approach was set at the low point in the wall where the Mycenaeans in the 13th century BC constructed a defensible entrance and their **famous Lion Gate** known by the triangular upper register picturing two facing lions with front paws on altars. From that point the citadel was reached by a steep ramp.

[See Pictures # 40 a & b – The Grand Entrance to Mycenae]

Immediately inside the wall and on the right side of the ramp **Heinrich Schliemann** (the man who discovered Troy by carefully following the descriptions in **Homer**) also found **Grave Circle A** here, which was the burial site of the royal family. In the process of excavation he uncovered 19 bodies in the tombs and he found 33 lbs. of golden artifacts in his work at Mycenae, perhaps the most famous of which is the so-called golden death mask of Agamemnon that is now in the Archaeological Museum in Athens. While many of the sections in the *Iliad* and the *Odyssey* are fantasy and reflect the folk tales of the bards who repeated the *Trojan cycle*, it is clear that the poet whom we refer to as Homer writing sometime in the 9th or 8th centuries BC had done careful research. He knew his geography and the historical settings of the **House of Atreus** and he understood the Trojan War of the 13th century. To think, as people of our era sometimes do, that the ancients could not distinguish between myth and reality is a reflection not on them but on our lack of perception!

[See Pictures # 41 a & b – The Royal Burial Circle (A) at Mycenae]

The size of the city to the contemporary visitor may seem a little small for the large population that would have lived in Mycenae at **height of its glory** but it is important to remember that the nobility lived inside the walls and the others lived on the outside. The uncovering of Grave Circle B which is outside the wall reminds us that even most of the nobility during the prosperous years of Mycenae were entombed outside the wall. Moreover, the discovery in the upper part of a secret stairway that led to a cistern and to a way of escape is an indication that the royal family knew that the city was not invulnerable.

Finally, one of the unique places to see in visiting Mycenae is the so-called **Treasury of Atreus** which was a *tholos* **tomb** in which the king was buried. Constructed of brick-like blocks of 33 concentric circles that gradually move inward until it reached a dome, the tomb takes the shape of a bee hive with a huge doorway, all of which was then covered with earth to form a mound. After preparation, the body of the king was then laid "in state" at the center. In the event that the *tholos* would be reused, an alcove was built at the side which could serve as an ossuary.

Epidaurus: (12)

Traveling east and south from Mycenae one soon arrives at Epidaurus, a town that is situated close to the Greek coast. The site is known today mainly because it has the **best preserved ancient theater** in Greece, seating about 12,000 and is still used today. It was designed by the younger **Polykleitus** at the end of the 4th century and was constructed in two stages (3rd and 2nd centuries BC). It has a wonderful circular orchestra of about 66 ft. (20 m.) in diameter and at the center there once stood an altar of Dionysus. The acoustics are so magnificent that visitors are usually astounded by the fact that a coin dropped in the orchestra can be heard in the top rows of the theater. The grand stage (*proskenion*) is more than 70 ft (22 m.) long and it has a permanent skene.

[See Picture # 42 – The Best Preserved Greek Theater at Epidaurus]

The reason for its excellent condition relates to the fact that the setting was extremely sacred to the ancients not only because of the number of **shrines** here (to Apollo, Artemis and Themis) but more particularly to **Asclepius,** god of healing whose mother died in child birth and who was brought up and learned his art of healing from his animal-like caretakers. Epidaurus was regarded as one of the greatest healing centers of Greece and people came from long distances to receive **healing**. According to the tradition, persons seeking healing were expected to stay overnight in the Abaton (hotel) and as they **slept non-poisonous snakes** in the place were expected to provide them with a diagnosis of their illness in a dream or a vision. Nearby was were thermal springs that were then along with other treatments expected to administer healing.

Olympia: (d)

In contrast to the large number of persons who visit the non-biblical sites of Mycenae and Epidaurus on the Peloponnese, the numbers of those who visit Olympia are rather small. Even though Olympia was exceedingly important in the history of Greece, it lies considerably to the west of the usual tourist traffic in the Peloponnese. But it would be an unfortuate oversight not to include some mention of this significant religious sanctuary and athletic venue which was a dominant center in Greek thinking for a millennium.

As one might suppose Olympia is linked to the name of Mt. Olympus, the dwelling place of the twelve primary gods of the Greek Pantheon (See the discussion in the Introduction). As in most of Greece, mountains play an important role in its history and the development of its myths. The mountain near Olympia is named Mt, Chronos and those familiar with the Greek primordial myth should immediately recognized that the two primordial deities/realities were known as *Chronos* (time/sky) and *Gea/Rhea* (earth/matter). These primary realities produced the twelve gods of the pantheon with Zeus as the king or lord of the realm. It should not surprise one therefore that the great Temple of Zeus (fifth century BC) became the central shrine of Olympia. This temple (210 x90 feet) was surrounded by a series of halls, porches, monuments, fountains, a Heroon (a shire honoring a hero or heroes) and included several smaller shrines primarily to Gea/Rhea and Hera (which was one of the oldest temples at the site, seventh century BC). As one might imagine, the female figures in Greek mythology usually were more comforting than their male counterparts and therefore were more attractive to the people who usually worshipped at those shrines.

Attached to the Olympian shrine complex was an athletic center which developed in importance alongside of the religious center and was enhanced by a myth as well. In the myth Heracles, the son of Zeus, was said to have lined out the parameters of the sacred grove (the Altis) which became the stadium (about 600 ft or 192 meters in length) where the Olympic contests would be held and it is said that he was responsible for the initiation of the Olympic Games to honor his father. In addition to the stadium there was a large athletic center, a gymnasium, an aquatic center (for swimming, etc), a bath house and other amenities and of course a hippodrome which has since been inundated by the nearby river.

As in the case of other major sanctuaries like Delphi, the site of Olympia was endowed with a number of "treasuries" where cities deposited votive offerings to the gods for past blessings both personal and corporate such as health and wealth and in gratitude for victories over opponents. Naturally petitions were also accompanied by gifts and the result was that Olympia became a wealthy center.

In terms of history, the kings of Pisa (See the myth concerning the Peloponnese above) and Elis initiated contests in honor of Zeus between their cities and at least by the middle of the fifth century BC these games had developed into an established tradition for Greece and its colonies every four years. The Delphic Oracle had been consulted during the period of almost continual warfare among the city states and the oracle advised that the permanent honoring of the Olympic Games would alleviate conflict. A sacred truce was declared during the time of the games in honor of Zeus which was guaranteed by Sparta, the strongest city state in the Peloponnese. Athletes were required to pledge their integrity during the athletic competitions in front of the great statue of Zeus which was situated near the Bouletarian (Council).

The first Olympiad was held in 776 BC and became the basis for the development of a reliable calendar which marked the time by the Olympiad and the years and months in between by the numbers 1to 4. The contests began with the first full moon of the summer solstice in honor of Zeus and they continued until AD 393 when Emperor Theodosius I declared them to be pagan festivals. Theodosius II then ordered the destruction of the Temple of Zeus in the fifth century.

Sparta: (e) I pause here briefly to mention in passing Sparta because almost everyone who knows a little about Greece is aware of Sparta's significant role in the Persian and Peloponnesian Wars and the important conflicts between Sparta and Athens.

The ancient Spartan community was highly organized into distinct classes of people. Those of Dorian ancestry were the elite and were the Spartans. Those of the earlier inhabitants were designated as Helots (slaves) and were forced to serve the elite class. Those from elsewhere were generally respected and known as *periokoi* (friends or neighbors), unless they became enemies and were subsequently conquered and enslaved. The life of the Spartans was highly regulated and both boys and girls were expected to be highly disciplined physically and athletically. Boys were taken from their homes at the age of seven and subjected to intense training to be warriors, including beatings to ensure their toughness.

There is very little for archaeologists to uncover of the ancient city Sparta since it was never fortified even though it was a powerful city state. Its importance waned after it was defeated by Thebes in 371 BC. It remained a local center during the period of the Romans but was decimated by the invading forces from the north in the late Byzantine period.

CHAPTER 3

VISITING THE GREEK ISLANDS

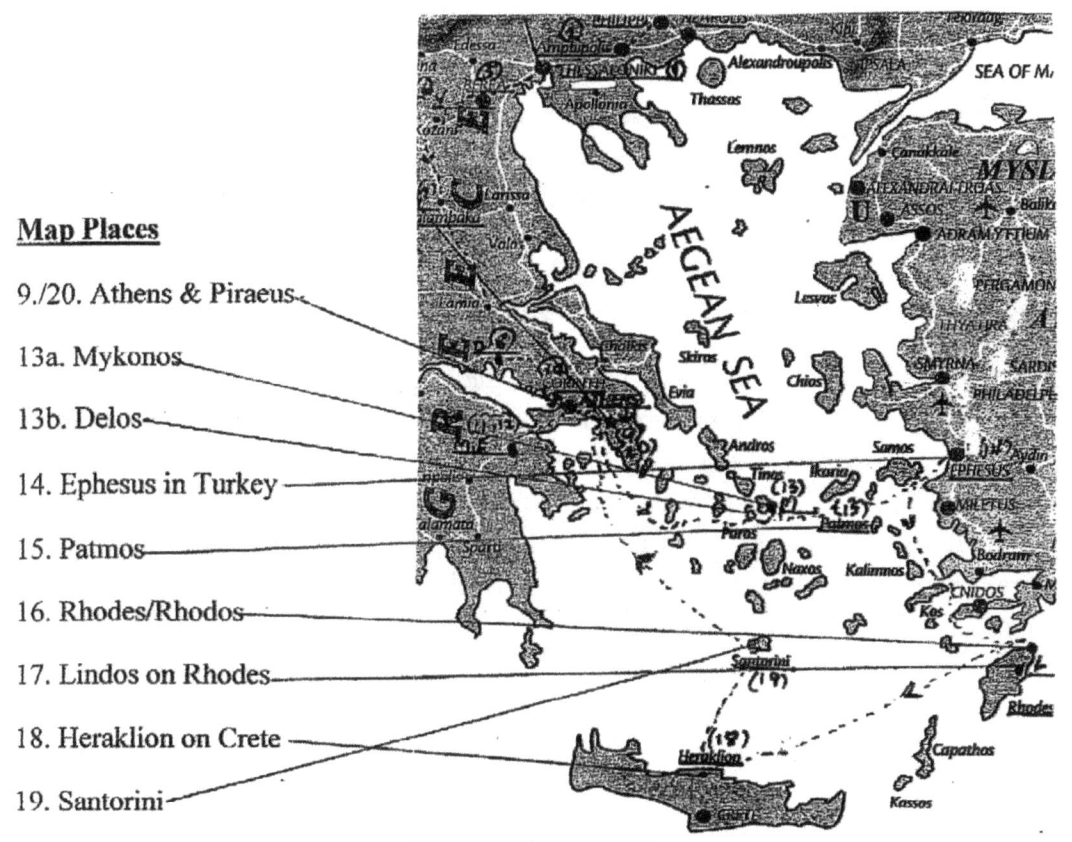

Map Places

9./20. Athens & Piraeus

13a. Mykonos

13b. Delos

14. Ephesus in Turkey

15. Patmos

16. Rhodes/Rhodos

17. Lindos on Rhodes

18. Heraklion on Crete

19. Santorini

DEPARTING THE MAINLAND

Piraeus: **(9, 20)** Voyages to the Greek islands normally begin in Piraeus, the **historic seaport** of Athens and one of the largest ports in the Mediterranean. At the beginning of the 5th century BC Themistocles, following the victory over the Persians, recognized the strategic importance of protecting the connection between the seaport and the city and initiated the building of an extended **security wall** of about 5 miles (8 km) between the two places. During the Peloponnesian war at the end of the century, however, the Spartans breached the wall and left the connection vulnerable. The Athenians repaired it at the beginning of the 3rd century but it was finally destroyed by Sulla during his sacking of Athens in 86 BC. As Athens shrunk in importance, the port also became less significant. Today, however, it is exceedingly significant and actually has **three harbors** to handle the large volume of both products and passengers. The Athens underground rail system is also connected to Piraeus.

B. THE CYCLADES ISLANDS, Part 1.

Mykonos and Delos: **(13 a, b)** Most voyages to the Greek islands stop at the small **picturesque** island of **Mykonos** for purposes of dining, rest and relaxation. Climbing the hill on the right side of the island near the harbor takes the visitor to a group of **windmills** which have been the subjects of many photographs and paintings. It has little historical significance for our purposes except for its little museum which contains some rare items including a two handled clay *pithos*, probably from the 7th century BC, which depicts segments from the battle of Troy and the earliest known representation of the Trojan Horse. It has a number of beaches for tourists including places for sunbathing in the altogether.

[See Pictures # 43 -- The Harbor & # 44 -- The Windmills of Mykonos]

For those who have the time Mykonos serves as the staging place for a short boat ride to the neighboring island of **Delos (Dilos)** which is one of those **magnificent ancient religious sites** that for a short time vied with Delphi (see above) in importance among the Greeks. It was believed to be the birth place for the twin gods Apollo and Artemis. Colonized by Ionians around 1000 BC, it became the head of the **Ionian League** from the 7th century until the **Athenians** came to power and declared the island to be **sacrosanct.** They forbad living and burial on the island in 425 BC and, indeed, insisted that the many bodies which had been buried there be removed to the nearby uninhabited island of Rinia (Rheneia) when the purification law concerning Delos was promulgated. After Athens came under Macedonian authority (314 BC), however, the strictures on Delos were loosened and settlement began again. Then under the Romans (168 BC) the island was granted a free status and prospered, but after being **looted** by Mithridates of Pontus (88 BC), it did not recover and in succeeding years its population shrunk to virtually nothing. Today it is basically a marvelous **archaeological preserve** containing the remains of great houses, shrines, the ruins of a theater, and three temples to Apollo; but with no hotels. Visitors to the island are expected to leave the island before night. The museum here is quite good but the most important finds have been taken to the Archaeological Museum in Athens.

C. THE DODECANES ISLANDS

Patmos: **(15)** Visiting the island of Patmos is of special interest to most Christians who have studied the **Book of Revelation** and remember that John received his vision here and wrote the Apocalypse (Book of Revelation) as a message of hope and warning to the churches of Asia.

Patmos is the smallest (13 sq. miles) and the most northerly of the Dodecanese Islands in the Aegean Sea. Arrival here is either by a cruise ship from Athens or by a ferry from

Ephesus/Kusadasi in Turkey (Asia Minor). It is for the most part a narrow, rocky, volcanic bit of land with a hook in the north which is the only area with a fair amount of arable soil. But like most of the Greek islands, it has a rather **hash beauty** and is a place which many Greeks today find attractive for vacationing.

The island was reportedly settled by Dorians and then by Ionians and served as a kind of outpost for the inhabitants of **Miletus** but not much mention of it is made in the ancient writers. We do know that the Romans exiled people to a number of the Greek islands but our basic information concerning Patmos as place of banishment or imprisonment comes to us from Revelation 1:9.

In my first visit to the island many years ago, I rode a donkey from the port of Khora (Hora; sometimes called Patmos) up the steep hill to what is now the little town of Skala and then to the famous monastery (*Hagias Ioannis*) which was founded in AD1088 to honor John, the writer of Revelation. The founder, a monk named Christodoulos (meaning: servant of Christ) Latrenus from the historic city of Nicaea, received the approval of the then emperor Alexios I Commenos to build the monastery on this island which had suffered from many raiding parties and pirates so that it was almost deserted. It is reputed to have been built over a earlier Christian church which in turn was constructed over an earlier Temple of Artemis.

[See Pictures # 45 and 46 -- The Monastery of St. John & The Famous Bell Tower on Patmos]

There are two important places to visit here. The first is the huge **fortified** monastery of St John with its 17th century church and its earlier chapel dedicated to Christodoulos with the marble sarcophagus of the founder, the dining hall with its 900 year old **frescoes**, the charming **bell tower** and the treasury, library or museum containing some valuable early manuscripts which are normally open to tourists.

[See Picture # 47 -- The Grotto Entrance, Traditional Site of John's Visions for Revelation]

The second important place is the **Cave of the Apocalyse** which is down the hill from the monastery in the town of Skala. The guide will normally pause before entering the cave to point out the small mosaic over the door which pictures **John with Prochorus**, his alleged scribe. While the New Testament does not indicate such a relationship, the Eastern Church espouses such a tradition concerning Prochorus who is mentioned in Acts 6:5. The cave which is framed with a chapel built by Christodoulos in 1090 in honor of St. Anne (either/or both (?): the mother of Mary or the mother of Christodoulos). Inside the chapel/cave the guide may suggest that a three finger crack in the ceiling occurred when God delivered his message to John and it represents the Trinity. The chapel screen or iconostasis contains three icons to **Mary, Christ and Anne**. Elsewhere are several other icons; the most notable being one of John receiving the Revelation. The site is worthy of pausing to reflect on the role of God in the history of world and what Christ was trying to communicate through his servant John.

[See Picture # 48 -- Fresco of the Vision on the Wall of the Grotto or Cave]

In the Footsteps of Paul and John

Today with many tourists visiting the site, buses transport visitors most of the way up the steep grade and then there are short walks to the monastery and the cave.

Rhodes (Rodos) and Lindos: (16, 17)

The island of Rhodes, lying 12 miles (19 km.) from the coast of Asia Minor, is one of the great tourist centers of the Mediterranean basin and the city of Rhodes itself is not only the capital of the island but the capital of the Dodecanese chain of islands. Because of its location and its natural harbors, it has attracted merchants and traders over the centuries. Indeed, during the 4th century BC it led the entire area in trade and its **rhetorical center** attracted politicians and philosophers from near and far. The Odeon which seated nearly 800 people was used by the philosophers and the rhetoricians in their teaching and orations. During the Roman period the school attracted important people to study there like Pompey, Julius Caesar, Cato and Cicero, to name only a few.

Rhodes also encouraged the arts and the development of great **sculptors** like Agesander and Polydorus but perhaps the most famous artistic achievement to emerge from Rhodes was the great bronze **Helios Colossus** (one of the ancient wonders). The statue was commissioned to celebrate the breaking of the siege of Demetrios Poliorcetes from Macedon in 305 BC. Standing about 98 ft. (c.29 m.) in height plus a pedestal, it was traditionally said to be erected in the harbor as a symbol of eternal Rhodian strength where the two columns are now standing but more likely it was erected in the court of the Helios Temple near the harbor. It was not eternal, however, and was felled by an **earthquake** which also destroyed much of the city in 227 BC.

[See Picture # 49 – Harbor of Rhodes (Site of the Colossus?)]

During the political struggles in Rome, Rhodes took the side of **Caesar** and as a result **Cassius** looted it of many treasures. Following the **Battle of Actium** and the defeat of Mark Antony in 31 BC **Herod the Great** who had been a friend of Antony quickly went to Rhodes to pledge his allegiance to Octavian (later Augustus) and was confirmed in his position as king of the Roman province of *Palestina*.

[See Picture # 50 – The Gigantic Crusader Fortress of Rhodes]

In the succeeding years Rhodes experienced a series of battles that left it weak until the time of the **Crusaders** who established their headquarters here after their defeat in the land of Israel. These Europeans warriors built a **great fortress** at Rhodes and were frequently referred to as the Knights of St. John. The fortress which still stands today had stout walls and with sections in the Knight's quarter called Inns or areas which were assigned to various countries/groups (or **"tongues,"** e.g. Italy, France, England, Spain, Germany, etc.). Other quarters were assigned to the wealthy supporters and politicians, the merchants and the general population.

[See Pictures #51 and 52 – Two Facades of the Crusaders Nations (Hostels/Tongues)]

From this fortress and its harbor, the Crusaders harassed the Muslim ships until the Ottoman ruler Suleiman (**Suleyman**) **the Magnificent** finally had enough and laid siege to the fortress, finally forcing the Crusaders to surrender and return to Europe. A core group of the **Knights of St. John** who had run the hospital, however, retreated to Malta and established themselves as an international medical organization. The island remained under Turkish domination until the Italians stretched their muscles and rested it from the Turks in 1912. Rhodes along with the other Dodecanese Islands was ceded to Greece in 1948 after World War II.

After delivering his farewell address to the Ephesian elders at Miletus, Acts 21:1 indicates that **Paul** then headed for Rhodes. The ship on which he was sailing apparently stopped at Rhodes before Paul went on his way to Jerusalem prior to his imprisonment. But although the text says nothing concerning his stop or the harbor where he landed, a tradition developed that he landed at the harbor in Lindos and that Paul established a church there. Such a tradition is an argument from silence and can not really be either asserted or disproved at this point.

Visitors to the island will find the great **fortress** at Rhodes to be fascinating as they walk the streets where the Inns of the various "tongues" were located. The Hospital of the Knights now serves as the **Archaeological Museum** (containing items such as the beautiful 1st century BC statue of Aphrodite) and is worth seeing just as is the Archbishop's Palace built in the 15th century AD.

[See Pictures # 53 - Acropolis at Lindos & # 54 - St Paul's Harbor at Lindos on Rhodes]

But perhaps the most interesting place to visit on Rhodes is **Lindos** with the **magnificent acropolis** and its ancient temple at a height of just over 500 ft. which overlooks the harbor named after St. Paul. The ascent is a little steep but there are resting places along the way and at each of the levels there are some excellent archaeological examples of buildings and items from the 4th and 2nd centuries BC as well as the 15th and 16th centuries AD. A visit to this site is a memorable event.

[See Pictures # 55 - Shops line the Streets of Rhodes &
 # 56 - Copies of Ancient Pottery on Sale in Rhodes]

Moreover, most people enjoy strolling the streets of the capital of Rhodes and bargaining in the seemingly countless shops within the walls of the great fortress.

D. CRETE

When one leaves Rhodes and heads back to Athens by ship, the major island on the way is Crete.

Crete (Kriti): **(18)** Crete is the largest of the Greek islands, nearly 165 miles (260 km.) long and it varies between about 10 to 40 miles wide with several different mountain ridges, the highest being Mt. Ida which rises to 8,058 ft.(2,456 m.). It is situated about 60 miles (95 km.) south of the Peloponnese. Today it has a population of about a half million people and its capital of Khania is on the northwest shore while its largest city is **Heraklion** (Iraklion/ Candia or ancient **Knossos**).

The history of Crete is so encrusted with layers of **myth** and fact so that one must take great care not to dismiss the legends as completely unreliable or as fantasy. One of Crete's primary legends asserts that **Zeus** was born in one of the mountain caves and who in the form of a mature bull later seduced Europa, the daughter of Tyros (the Phoenician King). She reputedly then born him three sons (Minos, Rhadamanthus and Sarpedon) who became the three rulers at Knossos, Malia and Phaistos as well as the progenitors of the Cretan inhabitants. Particularly at **Knossos** (in the center of Crete) the myth continued to expand and develop because **King Minos** was so focused on gaining wealth that he was given the **"golden touch"** but what seemed to be a blessing may actually have turned out to be a curse (cf. the comparable myth associated with **Midas from Sardis**). The riches of the Minoans was legendary and one reason for their wealth was that they developed a **medium of exchange** in the form of **ingots** which were exchanged rather than relying on the the older battering system. This medium of exchange was later surpassed by Croesus of **Sardis** who developed **coins** as the basis for trade.

What is crucial for contemporary people to understand is that Minos is probably not merely the name of one King; it is more likely the title for the priestly kings of Knossos. Now the more one reads and understands the ancient myths, the more one begins to understand that most of them are usually related to historical events or realities and as they were told, they were also meant to convey lessons to listeners (and later readers). Heinrich Schliemann recognized this fact and that is the reason he was able to use Homer to discover both Troy and Mycenae when most scholars thought Homer was just writing fanciful stories and not conveying the historical realities in the legends of the bards.

It is very clear that the ***Minoan period***, which emerged in Crete prior to Mycenae Age on the mainland, flowered not only considerably earlier than the Mycenaeans but it was one of the most highly advanced and wealthy cultures in the ancient world.

[See Pictures # 57, 58 and 59 – Reconstructions and Restorations by Arthur Evans of the Knosis Palace, the Royal Chambers & the Sophisticated Cooling System in Heraklion]

But it disappeared very quickly -- which has led to a great deal of **speculation**. Some have argued that its demise was the result of a harsh military intervention from Athens but more often it has been linked to the volcanic explosion on the nearby island of **Santorini** (Thira; see below) and/or a serious clash of the tectonic plates causing a series of major earthquakes in that area which devastate the country.

It is thought that the inhabitants of Crete first came from Africa perhaps in the 5th or 4th millennia BC and that about the middle of the 3rd millennium they were joined by others from Asia Minor. Artifacts uncovered in the palaces (noted above) point to their construction about the beginning of the 2nd millennium (c. 2000 BC). These palaces were then destroyed about 200 years later (the reason is unclear) but they were soon rebuilt. Then Knossos became the **center of power** and the Minoans gained the ascendancy. During this period construction of buildings with innovative facilities such as running water and sophisticate cooling systems were developed at Knossos. Viewing the superb museum at Heraklion, it is evident that artistic work genuinely flourished in this period and that pottery reached a level of great **beauty and sophistication** not evident in Greece prior to the rise of the Minoans.

While the ancient Minoans were not only an intelligent and sophisticated people, stories have come down to us indicating that, like many others in ancient times, they were also ruthless and extracted heavy toll on those whom they conquered. One of the great myths related to the Minoans concerns the story of the Minotaur, the half bull-half person monster who devoured people. According to the myth, Poseidon granted Minos the island of Crete in return for offering him the famous white bull. But Minos provided a substitute bull instead. Therefore, Posiedon punished him by placing lust in his wife for the bull and from that union the Minotaur was born. The monster was kept in a labyrinth but demanded human sacrifice. As the story proceeds, when the Minoans conquered Athens the legendary King Minos demanded that in addition to paying them tribute that the Athenians should send every nine years seven noble young virgins and a comparable number of young men. The Athenian theory was that the youths would be forced to enter a maze and would be devoured because they could not find their way out. The Athenian myth then details that Theseus, the young prince of Athens, agreed to be one of the youth and Ariadne, the daughter of Minos, became enamored with Theseus and supplied him with a long thread so that he could find his way out of the labyrinth. Theseus entered the labyrinth slew the Minotaur and after finding his way out, he carried the Princess to Athens as his bride.

[See Picture # 60 - The Royal Bull, the symbol of Minos and the Minoans which is also related to Zeus and to Ancient Mythology]

Now, as I indicated earlier, myths need to be understood as providing insight into early history and this myth is no exception. Let me challenge you my reader to reflect on this myth with me for a moment. Minos was quite likely the symbol for the Minoan leadership and the Minotaur could very likely be the Athenian perspective concerning the beastly toll that was being extracted from them by on the Minoans. The bull would naturally be regarded by the Athenians at this time as a harsh demanding god since he was thought to have come from Crete. The labyrinth could easily represent the incredibly complex of buildings of the sophisticated Minoan palace which would have seemed like a huge maze of buildings to the early Athenians who at that time hardly had developed much in the way of such construction patterns. We must remember that the Minoan culture predated the great buildings of Athens by almost a millennium.

[See Pictures # 61 - The Refurbished Throne Room & # 62 - Large Storage Jars in the Palace of Knosos]

To enter such the maze of Heraklion would certainly have seemed to the unsophisticated Athenians like a completely enveloping experience. But the Athenians would some day learn the secrets of building from others and particularly from both the Myceneans and their earlier counterparts, the fabled Minoans who were real people and not merely figures in mythical stories.

[See Pictures from the Heraklion Archaeological Museum # 63 & 64 – Memorial Minoan Axheads & Minoan Block Currency]

Sometime between the middle of the 15th and the early part of the 14th centuries BC, however, calamity struck (whether in one event or more is still not clear) and the Minoans never recovered their vitality. Within two centuries the Dorians in particular were immigrating in numbers to Crete, appropriating the prized sections of land and gaining ascendancy over the earlier Minoans who faded into the hills.

[See Picture # 65 -- Statues of the Great Myth of the Abducted Persephone, Pluto and the Guardian of Hades: Cerebus, the Three-headed Dog]

Rome seized the island in 67 BC and made Gortyna on the southwest coast the capital of Crete. Then, when the Empire was divided, Crete was ceded to Constantinople and the Byzantine rulers (AD 395). Crete fell to the **Arab forces in 824** and the major seaport of Rabd-el-Kandak (later Heraklion), very near the former city of Knossos, once more became the capital. The island became a **constant battle ground** among the Byzantines, Venetians and Genoese for over eight hundred years until the Turks conquered it in 1669 and violently suppressed the rebellious Cretans. The Cretans continued their resistance, regained their freedom and became a part of Greece again in 1913. The **Turks were bitterly hated** and were then driven out of the country in 1923.

As far as the New Testament is concerned, **Paul (as a prisoner)** landed temporarily at a small port in Crete called ***Kaloi Limenes*** (Acts 27:8) which can be translated as "Good Landings" (Fair Havens or Harbor) but since it was not a significant port, the centurion who knew that winter storms were coming was determined to move to the larger port of Phoenix. He would not listen to Paul's warning and as a result the ship encountered the famous wind ***Euroqulo*** (Acts 27:14 -- usually translated as "northeastern" but like our naming of hurricanes, it was regarded as a horrible storm with mythical implications) which whistles down the Adriatic and the ship was wrecked off the island of Malta.

Titus, a Gentile (Gal 2:3), is also mentioned as having been a missionary in Crete and when Paul writes to him he quotes a popular but very unfavorable maxim concerning the Cretans which is probably attributable to **Epimenides**, a Cretan philosopher from the 6th century BC, as being "always liars, evil beasts and lazy gluttons" (Titus 1:12). The statement is of course a serious over-generalization but it points to the strong independent and irritating spirit which many outsiders experienced in the Cretans and which later conquerors found extremely hard to control and subjugate. While few tourists on cruises stop at Gortyna it is important to mention it here not merely because it was the Roman political capitol of the island but also because traditions indicate that it was the ministry center for Titus on the island and the place of his martyrdom. The archaeological ruins are also significant here.

While the reconstructions of Knossos by Sir **Arthur Evans** have been criticized by some archaeologists as being a little skewed, walking through the reassembled remains of the Palace complex at Knossos is for most visitors a significant experience of **reentering the past** (seeing the throne room, the quarters of the royals, the facilities of the palace, etc.) because it provides an impressive sense of how people of wealth lived during the height of the Minoan period. Then to visit the wonderful **museum** in Heraklion and pause before the genuinely unique artifacts and the artwork of this very sophisticated culture is to gain an important appreciation for a truly magnificent past generation.

E. THE CYCLADES ISLANDS, Part 2.

Santorini (Thira): **(19)** Finally, on most cruises to the Greek islands one of the highlights has to be visiting the volcanic Greek island of Thira (Santorini) at the southern end of the Cyclades Islands.

[See Picture #66 – Anchored in the Volcanic Bay of Thira/Santorini]

About the middle of the 2nd millennium, the **volcanic island literally exploded** and the sea rushed in while the cone dropped into the center of the crater and the result was the formation of a huge sheltered bay that one can observe today. The impact of the explosion must have been catastrophic for the entire region. Furthermore, the island of Thira lies almost directly **north of Crete** and of Knossos, the capital city of the Minoans. When the volcano exploded undoubtedly a **giant tsunami** must have been created and the cataclysmic results which followed could easily have wiped out all the Minoan towns and villages along the coast, to say nothing of the harbor and the capital city of Knossos which would have been directly in its path. Until recently not many people in our generation had experienced the great devastation which can be caused by a tsunami but in our lifetime we no longer need much explanation of such a phenomenon. Most of the scholars that had earlier questioned the possible impact of such a tsunami on Crete probably do not now have the same doubts they had previously expressed.

The history of Santorini is linked to the **rise of the Minoan culture** and it remained virtually uninhabited after the volcanic explosion until around 1000 BC when the Dorians began to settle there. It began to develop as an important transit station for the Athenians in the 5th century and after *Alexander G*, the **Ptolemies** established a naval outpost here to protect their trading ships between Egypt and the eastern Mediterranean until Romans took firm control especially after the defeat of Antony and Cleopatra at **Actium in 31 BC**. In the Middle Ages the **name Thira was changed to Santorini in honor of St. Irene**, (Santa Irene) the patron of the island. During this period the island was held primarily by Venice until it was taken by the Turks in 1537. It was liberated along with other Greek islands when the western Europeans faced-off with the Turks in 1912-13 and ultimately returned it to Greece.

[See Pictures # 67 & 68 – The Gondola for Ascending the Volcano's Wall & A View of the City and Bay from the Top]

As indicated earlier, visiting Santorini is a delightful experience. Ships do not normally dock at the island, but **lower their anchors in the sheltered bay** of the fractured volcanic cone. The water in places here is nearly 1,300 ft. (390 m.) deep. **Smaller boats taxi people** from the ship to the various havens around the bay. The main dock at Skala is near to an **elevator tram** that, for a small price, carries people up the steep side of volcano to the small town of Thira at the top which is over 1,100 ft (330 m.) above the water below. If one prefers, it is possible to climb the many steps or ride a donkey to the top, but one should be prepared for the fact that the animals do not smell like perfume. The **view** from the top is spectacular and the village, with its many tourist shops and restaurants, provides adequate opportunity for shopping, browsing and taking memorable pictures.

[See Pictures # 69 & 70 -- The Beautiful Orthodox Church on Santorini: Exterior & Interior]

Approximately 10 miles (16 km.) from the present town around the island built on the slope and up to the acropolis are the ruins of the **ancient town of Thira** which was excavated by **Hiller von Gaertringen** at the beginning of the 20th century and which contains several shrines and temples to Dionysius, to Isis, and to Apollo, a grotto to Hermes and Hercules, two gymnasia, a theater and the agora. Also nearby are also several chapels and churches.

Concluding a visit to the Greek Islands with a stop at Santorini will leave a sense of fulfillment in one's mind and certainly a desire to return to follow elsewhere in the footsteps of Paul and John.

CHAPTER 4

VISITING WESTERN TURKEY/ANATOLIA

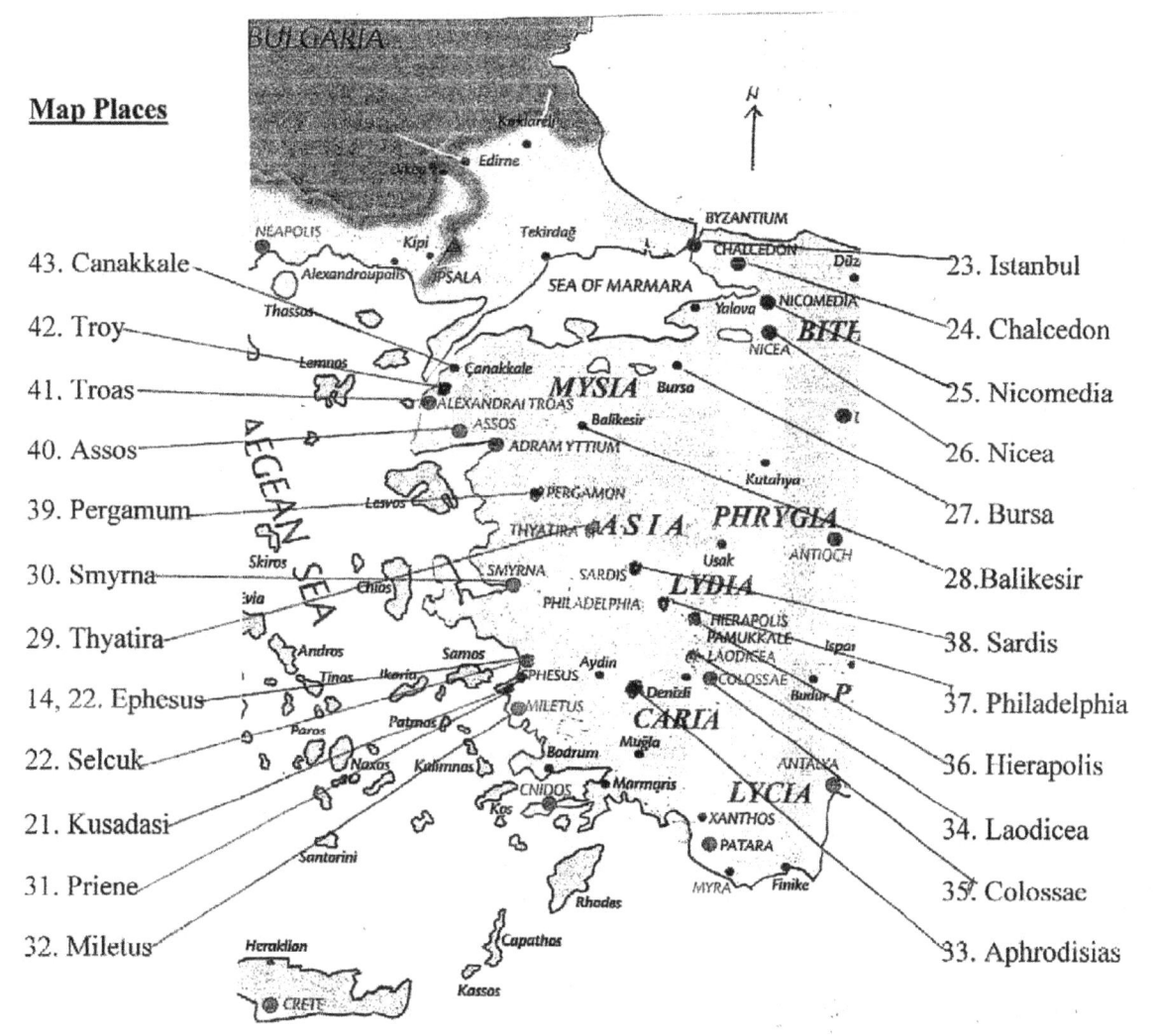

A. EPHESUS: THE LEADING CITY OF ANCIENT ASIA AND ITS CLOSE NEIGHBORS

For the sake of those travelers whose journey of following in the Footsteps of Paul and John brings them by ship only to Ephesus in Western Turkey, I have begun my reflections with a discussion of the magnificent archaeological site of Ephesus. I would, however, remind readers that a brief five hour stop in Ephesus with part of that time in a carpet shop is really an insufficient opportunity to grasp the immense significance of this magnificent ancient city and of the other treasured sites in Western Turkey.

Kusadasi: **(21)** While ancient Ephesus was a harbor city, it is today encrusted with silt so that those who arrive by ship in this area of Turkey today will land at the harbor of **Kusadasi.**

[See Picture # 71 – The Modern Harbor City of Ksuadasi]

Ephesus/Ayasoluk/Selcuk [9] : **(14, 22)** Mentioned in Acts 18-20; 1 Cor 15:32; 16:8; 1 Tim 1:3 and 2 Tim 1:18; 4:12; Rev 1:11; 2:1, Ephesus was a strategic **ancient seaport city** on the west coast of Turkey which today is situated inland about 4 miles because of the **silting** of the Cayster River. Lying in ruins about 40 miles south of the bustling harbor city of Ismir (ancient Smyna), near the modern town of **(33)** Selcuk and sheltered by the island of Samos, Ephesus is one of the most **phenomenal archeological sites** in the Mediterranean world.

Legend suggests that the "Amazons" built their town here because of its nearness to the birth site of the goddess who was designated as **"Mother Earth."** Then, at least a thousand years before Christ, Ephesus was captured from the Asian residents and established as Greek city by the Ionians (under **Androclus**, the prince of Athens). The Greeks adopted the local patron goddess **Cybele** and identified her with the Greek deity **Artemis**. Ephesus was then conquered and reestablished in the mid sixth century BC by Croesus and the Lydians who constructed a great temple to Artemis. The city and area was thereafter conquered by the **Persians** under Cyrus and later by *Alexander G* in 334 BC.

[See Picture # 72 – Statue of Artemis (Diana) in the Museum at Ephesus]

The **Temple of Artemis** (the Artemision) had suffered a tragic fire in 356 BC (allegedly on the day of Alexander's birth) so in order to gain the loyalty of the proud Ephesians, he offered to rebuild the Temple at his own expense. The Ephesian elders not wishing either to alienate or be indebted to *Alexander G* **responded** that it was not appropriate for one god to build a temple to another god. This response has become a classic example of walking a tight rope. Nevertheless, the historian Strabo (*Geog.* xiv.1. 22) suggests that the temple stood unfinished for another two centuries. As I indicated in my larger article, the statue of Artemis was seemingly **covered with breasts** (?) probably signifying her blessed productivity. Her main statute may also have been constructed in part from a fallen meteorite which could explain the text in Acts 20:35: "the sacred stone that fell from the sky." Although the Temple today lies in ruins with only one pillar standing where once there was a great temple, from our calculations it probably measured about 420x240 ft. (128 x73 m.) with 117 (not 127 according to Pliny) columns. The site of the temple seems to have been moved several times and its last location was about a mile from the city center. Typical of the **Romans**

---

[9] For more information on this site see G. L. Borchert, "Ephesus" in *The International Standard Bible Encyclopedia*, rev. ed., Vol. 2 (Grand Rapids: Eerdmans, 1982), 115-17.

who had alternative names for the Greek gods, the Romans honored Artemis as Diana. The statement of Pliny that "the sea used to wash up to the temple of Diana" (*Nat. his.* ii. 87 [201]) is probably a generalized statement concerning the city of Ephesus and may not be an accurate description of its specific site.

After the death of *Alexander G*, the city was assigned to Lysimachus (one of Alexander's generals) but it was soon rested from him by his fellow general **Selucus**, the ancestor of the Syrian house that troubled the Jews. Finally, the **Romans** defeated the powerful Selucid king Antiochus III in 189 BC and the area was entrusted to the rulers of Pergamum as protectors of the province of Asia for the Romans (Livy xxxvii. 36-45). Ephesus, however, continued to have a rather **independent** status with local **Asiarchs** in charge (cf. Acts 19:31). Indeed, it rebelled against Rome in 88 BC and it was not really brought under full control until it was subdued by **Mark Antony** in 44 BC. It flourished under **Augustus** and by the time John wrote the Book of Revelation the Romans had moved the **capital** of Asia from Pergamum to Ephesus. The city then became one of the major urban centers in the Roman Empire.

Not only was it a vibrant sea port, but it was also a divisional point for **inland traffic.** The city stood at the intersection of two major ancient highways: (1) the northerly axis from Miletus in the south to Pergamum and Troas (near ancient Troy) in the north, and (2) the westerly axis from Ephesus to Hierapolis/Laodicea/Colossae and on to Phrygia and Tarsus in the west. It was a wealthy, **cosmopolitan** city with people plying many trades.

[See Pictures # 73 & 74 -- The Facade from the Library of Celsus & An Imperial Temple]

The remains of the great marble street which was replete with many fountains (e.g. Trajan), baths and temples (e.g. Hadrian) and the magnificent **Library of Celsus** are still visible for the visitor. Interestingly, on the steps of the library is a carved **menorah**, the sign that Jews were also living there. Among its well-known residents was the early 5th century BC philosopher **Heraclitus**. And with so many sailors on shore leave while stevedores unloaded their cargos, it is natural that among the trades one might find signs of loose morals. Accordingly, one of the intriguing sights for the visitor is the **bare foot** which was carved into the walkway that was the ancient sign for the local brothel.

[See Picture # 75 -- An Ancient Bare Footprint -Sign of a Brothel]

But Ephesus also had a very special appeal to the ancients because of the annual **Artemision festival** which drew huge crowds of religious visitors to the magnificent **Temple, one of the seven wonders** of the ancient world. But it was more than a mere temple and since it was regarded as the most **sacrosanct** shrine in the eastern Mediterranean region, people deposited their savings there and entrusted their wealth to the sanctity of the religious center. Thus the city became the financial or **banking institution** of the entre region. To understand the hostility of the silversmiths to Paul's proclamation of the gospel (Acts 19:27), one must understand how protective the people were for the sanctity of their famous temple. It was the foundation of much of the business that transpired in Ephesus.

In the Footsteps of Paul and John

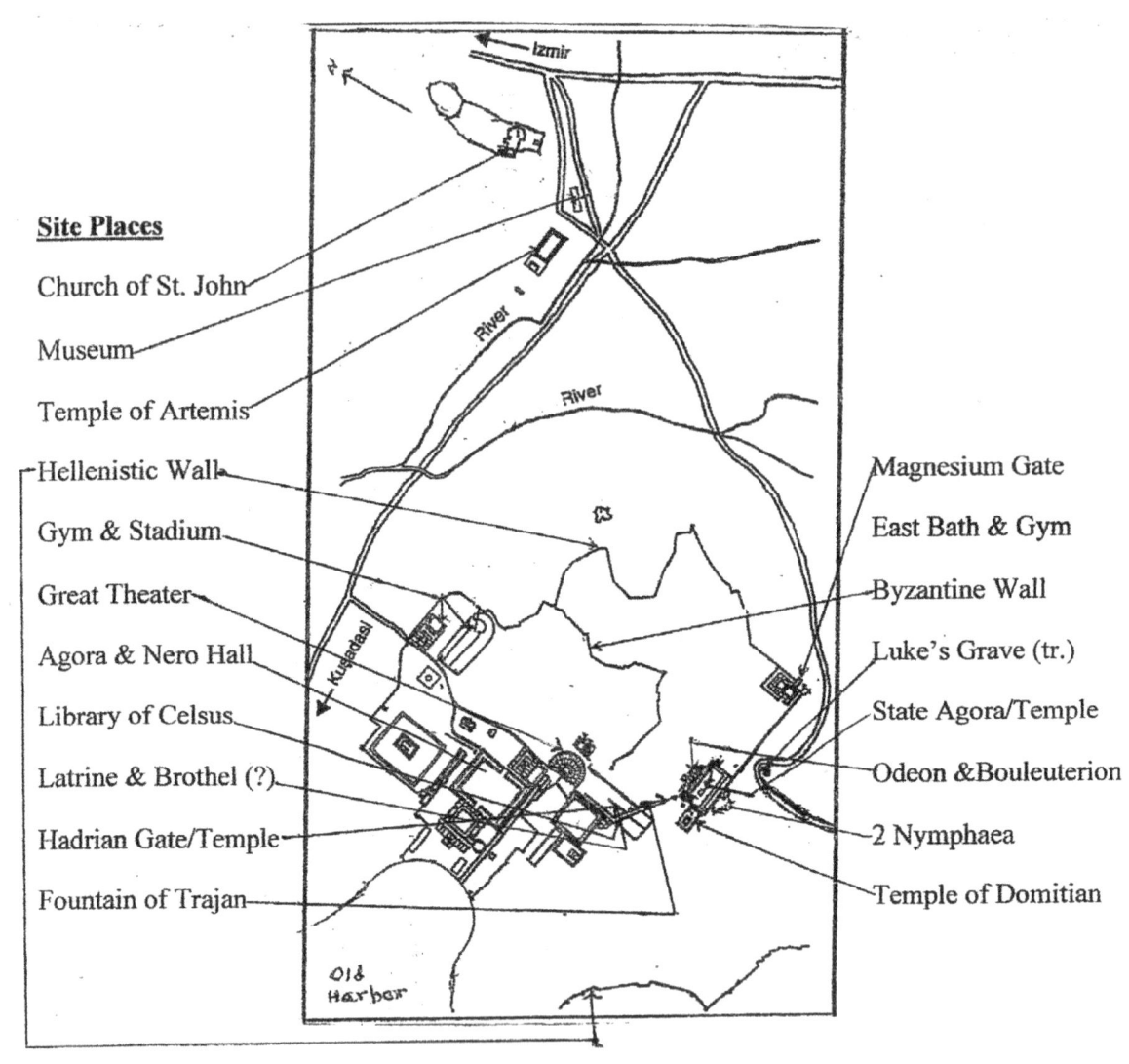

Site of Ancient Ephesus

The city's grand outdoor **theater** mentioned in the Acts story of the riot went through several reconstructions so that by the end of the 3rd century AD it could have accommodated at least 24,000 people with sixty-six tiers of seats. The huge stage measuring 70 ft. by 115 ft. was capable of handling almost any play and the acoustics in the theater are even today still phenomenal. Sections of the magnificent façade were constructed both in the first and third centuries.

[See Picture # 76 -- The Great Theater of Ephesus and the Colonnaded Way]

South of the theater in the higher section of the city is a great complex which includes the upper entrance to the city, the state agora/forum (market) including a temple usually designated to Julius

Caesar/Dea Roma, a smaller Odeon (for music and special addresses), several beautiful Nymphaea (fountains) and the Prytaneion (eternal fire of Hestia Boulania, the goddess of wellness). To the east were the great Magnesian Gate and a large gymnasium with a typical tri-section Hellenistic bathhouse (caldarium, tepidarium, and frigidarium)

[See Pictures # 77 – The Greek Goddess Niki (victory) Holding a Wreath and a Palm Branch(cf. Rev4:10 &7:9) & #78 – The Entrance to the Civic Agora]

Paul first visited the city on his second journey (Acts 18:19-28) and stayed there for at least two years on his third journey (19:8-10). He apparently founded a fairly strong church there because in the Book of Revelation it indicates that the people were a faithful group but like so many churches which start with great vitality it later lost its zest (first love) and became less vibrant and more **traditional**, remaining loyal to the faith but lacking its earlier zeal (cf. Rev 2:1-7). The Book of Revelation also identifies crowns (wreaths) and palm branches as symbols of honor and victory (cf. Rev 4:10 and 7:9), symbols that were familiar to the Greeks in Ephesus.

The city gained status in the second century under **Trajan and Hadrian** and it was recognized several times during succeeding years with the honorary title of *neokoros*, the **guardian** of the Temple to *Dea Roma* (the divine Rome).

[See Picture # 79 –An Ancient Fresco of Paul flanked by Thecla and her Mother Recently Discovered in a Cave above the site of Ephesus at Ayasoluk]

One of the interesting sites in ancient Ephesus is the cave high above the ancient city which was recently discovered containing a **fresco of Paul** in the middle with early converts, **Thecla and Thecla's mother**, on either side of him. Reaching the cave is a difficult climb and is open only with special permission from the authorities. The cave provides some support for the tradition that Thecla was an early supporter of Paul as indicated in the anonymous work entitled The *Acts of Paul and Thecla*[10] which was written in the late second century.

The **silting** of the harbor from the Cayster River, however, had serious consequences for the city and although several attempts were made to save the connection between the sea and the city by King Attalus Philadelphus and Emperor Hadrian, the repairs to the channel only provided temporary relief.

Ayasoluk/Selcuk: (22)

During the Byzantine era, the city of Ephesus moved from the harbor area to the slopes of the nearby foothills known as **"Ayasoluk"** which I have argued in my earlier article was probably derived from the Greek *hagios theologos* ("the holy theologian"), a designation used to describe John, the writer of the Gospel and the Book of Revelation who is to be regarded as the patron saint of Eastern Christianity. **Justinian**, perhaps the last of the great

---

[10] For those interested in consulting this work see the English translation of E Hennecke-W. Schneemelcher, *New Testament Apocrypha*, Vol. 2 (Philadelphia: Westminster, 1965), 353-64.

Christian emperors, constructed a **magnificent church** in this vicinity that is known as the **Basilica of St. John** (which is near the modern town of **Selcuk**).

[See Picture # 80 – The Basilica of St. John in Ephesus/Selcuck]

Many of the stones for the building of this church as well as for the even grander cathedral of St. Sophia (*Hagia Sophia*/ Aya Sofya -- "sacred wisdom") in Istanbul/Constantinople are said to have been scavenged from the nearby hitoric **Temple of Artemis**. Unfortuantely virtually nothing now remains of this amazing temple except **one pillar** in a large field which marks the area where once stood the **so-called grandest temple in the world, one of the seven ancient wonders, having 127 columns**, more than any other temple built.

In AD 431 undr the sponsorship of Emperor Theodosius II the city hosted the **Third Ecumenical Council** in the earlier of Church of Mary during the controversies concerning the nature of Christ and which condemned Nestorius both for his unwillingness to unite the two natures of Christ in his theology and for his refusal to recognize Mary as "the mother of God" (*theotokos*). A later minor council was also held in Ephsus in AD 449 in a dispute between the eastern and western churches over the views of **Eutyches** and the technical question of the blending of the two natures of Christ. This meeting served as a foretast of largest meeting of bishops up to that time who were summoned two years later to Chalcedon by Emperor Marcian for the Fourth Ecumenical Coucil. It is interesting to note that while only the shell of the great Church of St John remains standing today, the Orthodox Church in Turkey still maintains a major bishop's seat for Ephesus under the direct supervision of the Ecumenical Patriarch in Istanbul/Constantinople.

In concluding this brief discussion on Ephesus, the leading city of Asia in the past, we turn now to Istanbul, the major city of Turkey today.

B. ISTANBUL AND ITS ENVIRONS: THE ANCIENT-MODERN METROPOLIS *(For map of the Golden Horn see page 137)*

Byzantium/Constantinople/Istanbul. **(23)** Today Istanbul is by far the largest city in Turkey with a population in excess of 13 million. It is a world-class modern "Megapolis," the economic and cultural center of Turkey. It is a bi-continental city, spanning the Bosphorus which divides Europe from Asia. With approximately one third of its residents living on the Asian side, it is regarded as the second largest urban center in Europe. It was founded as Byzantium by Greeks in approximately 665 BC and it has functioned as the capital city of several empires: first as the empire of Constantine and then as the capital of the eastern or Byzantine empire when the Roman Empire was divided from the west in AD 395. It functioned for a brief period (1204-1261) during the time of the Crusaders as the capital of the so-called eastern Latin Kingdom and after 1453 and the fall of Constantinople to the Muslims it became the capital of the Ottoman Empire until the political upheavals led by the military in 1922. Today the capital of Turkey is not Istanbul but Ankara which is in central Anatolia. Yet Istanbul remains the leading city, the center for business, culture and learning with Ankara second and Ismir (ancient Smyrna) third, both far behind in size.

During the first century AD Byzantium stood as the Roman bulwark and free colony at the eastern end of the *Via Egnatia* providing a safe haven for those who had traveled through the more hostile region of Thrace from Macedonia to Bithynia and Pontus (provincial areas mentioned in 1 Peter 1:1). It likewise served as the guardian gateway for protecting the sea lanes stretching from the eastern lands around the Black Sea and beyond.

The City of Byzantium, according to the **ancient story**, was named after Byzas, a Greek who before he began his travels consulted the oracle at Delphi to learn of his future and was instructed to settle "Against the blind." When he reached the Bosphorus around 655-70 BC, he found a settlement on the Asian side near Chalcedon. But when he inspected the other side of the water (Europe) he found an ideal harbor in the vicinity of Golden Horn and he apparently exclaimed that the other settlers "must be blind." Thus was born the tradition concerning the founding of the ancient city of Byzantium. During the Roman period the city willingly joined Rome in its expansionism but it was sacked by Septimius Servus in AD 196 when it was caught in a Roman civil war. When the Byzantines reannounced their loyalties to the Roman imperium, the city was reestablished and renamed Augusta Antonio.

The City of Constantinople and the Eastern Empire. Constantinople became central to Christian history when in AD 330 Emperor Constantine officially **moved the capital** of the Roman Empire to the earlier Byzantine site from Rome. Scholars differ slightly on the beginning of the Byzantine Period but it can be dated as early as the initial plans for the moving the capital in 324, the holding of the Council of Nicea in 325 to the official establishment of Constantinople in 330.

But I believe it is important briefly to lay the **foundation** for this move before proceeding further. Constantine's father, **Constantius Chlorus**, who was the Roman governor of Britain, Gaul and Spain had not been much for the persecution of Christians so when he fully assumed the role of an emperor following the abdication of the persecutors of Christians –Diocletian and Maximian— he adopted the purple robe and took the tile of Augustus until he died in AD 306. **Constantine**, who had been the favorite son of Chlorus, was at that time in Britain and his troops proclaimed him Emperor. But at that point, there were often several rival emperors and Constantine had the task of rising above his rivals. He first took on Maxentius who relied on pagan magic as his basis for power. The story of Constantine's encounter with a **vision of the cross** is well-known and does not need to be further detailed here but relying on his vision he overcame all other challengers and defeated his final rival Licinius in 323. Then he turned his attention to the reality of government.

Two factors among others played a significant role in his plan for the empire. The first was his realization that **Christianity** could be a **powerful force** in building unity. Therefore, he issued his declaration of toleration concerning Christians and Christianity blossomed. He gave his mother **Queen Helena** authority to search out the holy sites related to the life and ministry of Jesus and she traveled throughout Israel establishing shrines where she could find traditions concerning Jesus and building chapels and churches at these sites so that Christian pilgrims could visit these revered places. He also supplied funds for the rebuilding and refurbishing of churches that had been destroyed or damaged during the period of persecution. But he was frustrated over the fact that Christian theologians argued vehemently over issues of the faith because he envisaged those arguments as being destructive of unity and peace in the empire. Accordingly, he instructed the theologians of the Church to meet together in a world-wide council of bishops and settle their disputes. Since Christians were more numerous in the eastern part of the empire, he summoned them to meet at the historic site of **Nicea in 325**. While the bishops frequently had earlier held smaller consultations to settle disputes, this **Ecumenical Council** was the first of the seven early major councils to be convened by emperors and it established a very close tie between the **church and the state**. One could argue that such a tie was a positive support for the spread of Christianity but that it also proved to be detrimental to the authenticity of the Christian faith. Since that time and the rise of the Free Church movement, many Protestants eschew such close ties between church and state.

The second major factor to be mentioned involves Constantine's **transferring the capital** of the Roman empire from Rome to the old city of Byzantium. Constantine was very familiar with the rising power of the hostile tribes north of Italy. Realizing the vulnerability of Rome in relation to the rising encroachments of the northern European tribes, Constantine believed it was appropriate to establish a new capital in the secure center of his empire and he renamed the place "Constantinople" (**the city of Constantine**). Constantine died in 337, a mere seven years after the founding of his new city. The move was regarded in Rome as quite divisive but the empire was so vast and sprawling that it had often had experienced previously the presence of at least two rulers in the empire who were regarded as emperors and that tradition would continue periodically even after Constantine and his sons. On the other hand, the move could be considered as quite a wise one because following the Constantinian era Rome and the western empire was battered repeatedly from the north and much of Europe was plunged into what has frequently been called the Dark Ages. While Attila the Hun threatened Constantinople and it was severely damaged by a severe earthquake during the Theodosian era in 447, the city was rebuilt and continued to survive. Indeed, during the reign of **Justinian** (527-65) it prospered and was greatly enhanced with such improvements as the complete rebuilding of the *Hagia Sophia* as the grandest cathedral in the empire.

[See Picture # 81 – Hagia Sophia: Justinian's Christian Cathedral]

The city and the eastern empire were threatened repeatedly by the growing powers among the Muslims in the south and suffered even from European Crusaders. These Crusaders in their efforts to "free the Holy Land" and retake territories from the followers of Mohamed also took Constantinople and established their headquarters here (and in such places as Rhodes and Caesarea Maritima) with the result that this city briefly became the capital of the so-called Latin Kingdom from 1206 to 1261. But it finally fell to the Ottomans in 1453 and the succeeding period will be discussed below.

The Christian Heritage in the City. In order to glorify the city which bore his name, Constantine removed treasures from a number of places throughout the empire and brought them to his city. Among those treasures that were scavenged during this early period and set up around the area now known as the Sultanahmet (the ancient city center) are the famous Serpentine Column which was removed from the Temple of Apollo in Delphi and was a memorial offering bearing the names of the Greek city states that participated in the battle of Platea (479 BC) in which the Persians were defeated. Also, included among the pirated treasures is the Egyptian Obelisk from the time of Thutmose III (1484— 1450 BC, one of the most famous warrior pharaohs[11]). Unfortunately, during transportation it was broken and only about one-third (the upper section) was mounted on a new pedestal in the area of **the ancient Hippodrome**. Nearby is also the column of Constantine which was originally fashioned prior to his reign but the base on which it stands reflects his family and deeds.

Northeast of the Hippodrome stands the great basilica known as the *Hagia Sophia* ("Holy/Sacred Wisdom"). The present church is the third structure on this site. The first was completed and consecrated during the reign of Constantius, the son of Constantine, in AD 360. After it was destroyed by fire in the tumult surrounding the exile of the great orator John Chrysostom in 409, Emperor Theodosius II ordered its reconstruction, but it too was later destroyed in 532 during a period of unrest. Emperor Justinian then undertook a new grand plan for its reconstruction, the first phase of which was completed in 537 and at that time it was the largest building in the world with a floor space much in excess of 190,000 sq ft. (or 21, 500 sq. yds./18,000 sq m.). The great dome rises to a height of 182 ft. above the floor and it contained many fine mosaics, some of which may still be seen today. The columns in this grand church are alleged to have been brought from ancient temples throughout the empire. We are quite certain that many of the stones (including the six well-known green columns) used in the building of this cathedral are from the Temple of Artemis in Ephesus (cf. a similar pattern of reusing the stones from Artemis was in the Church of St. John in Ephesus). This third structure remained the largest Christian Church until the construction of St. Peter's in Rome and it served as the site for the **Fifth and Sixth Ecumenical Councils** (AD 553 and 680; see the list of Councils in the Introduction). After the fall of the city to the Ottomans, the church was transformed into a mosque and many of the fine works of art were lifted, damaged or covered with paint. After the fall of the Ottomans, the *Hagia Sophia* has been turned into a museum and the building is gradually being restored.

It is also important here to mention in respect to the Constantinian period the significant *Hagia Eirene* (the church of "Holy/Sacred Peace"), frequently called the Church of St. Irene. Although it lies some distance from the Sultanahmet area, it should be noted that it was the site of the **Second Ecumenical Council** (AD 381) which reaffirmed the decisions of Nicea but also added the assertion of the divinity of the Holy Spirit and reasserted the rejection of Arianism and the view that the divine nature of Christ overwhelmed his human nature (See the earlier outline of Councils).

---

[11] For a brief listing of the most important Pharaohs, their dynasties and their deeds, see Gerald l Borchert, *The Lands of the Bible: Israel, the Palestinian Territories, Sinai and Egypt*, etc. (Cleveland, TN: Mossy Creek Press/ Parson's Porch, 2011), 121-25.

This church was the first Christian cathedral in the area and it was built on the site of an ancient Temple to Aphrodite. It was significantly consecrated during the reign of Constantine and although it suffered destruction in AD 532, it was rebuilt by Justinian and it has the distinction of not having been turned into a mosque.

A Brief Note on the Central Site of Orthodox Christianity. Constantinople has been the seat of the leading Patriarch of the Orthodox Communities. In the conflicts with Rome, the Patriarch there was singled out for recognition by the other Orthodox communities and endowed with the title of "the **Ecumenical Patriarch**." Rome countered with the designation of their Patriarch as "the Papa" or the Pope and referred to him as "the servant of the servants of God." While the Roman Patriarch is viewed by their constituency as an ultimate authority, the remaining Patriarchs throughout the Orthodox world (such as Russia, Egypt/Coptic, Syria, Armenia, etc) do not consider any Patriarch as ultimate or above the others in matters of faith and practice. Instead, they regard each Patriarch and each church as "autosephelous" (or self-governing). Thus, they consider the Ecumenical Patriarch to be primarily "**first among equals**." Decisions concerning faith and practice in Orthodoxy must be made in consultation or in Councils with each other, which also means that change comes very slowly in Orthodox communions.

In my visits to and inter-church discussion with the Ecumenical Patriarchate, it became quite clear to me that the Protestant Reformation and the Renaissance has hardly touched Orthodoxy. Instead, one gains this feeling far more than in conversations with the Vatican that one is stepping back a long way in time; indeed much further into the past with the Orthodox than with the Roman Catholics. One example may suffice as it concerns the great Nicene formulation or Creed. After the churches had in concert decided on the formulation of that confession, the Roman Patriarch inserted into the creed the well-known "*filioque* **clause**" insisting that the Holy Spirit proceeded not only from the Father but also from the Son since it seems from the statement in John 15:26-27 that both the Father and the Son have together sent the Spirit. But the eastern Patriarchs refused to agree to this addition insisting that the Roman formulation was revisionistic. That difference of opinion is crucial for understanding the importance of tradition within Orthodox thinking and it set the stage for the beginning of a major division in church unity since neither side refused to agree with the other and condemned the other.

Today the Ecumenical Patriarcate is housed in a rather small complex, far less auspicious than it was in the past or is currently evident in Rome. But with that statement, it is important to move on to the next stage of history with respect to the city.

The Modern Name of Istanbul is a construct derived from the Greek *eis ten polin* which means "in/into the city," a designation which basically refers to the city center. It has little historical significance but was a decision of the Turkish government in March of 1930 after the Revolution which had deposed the Ottomans and sought to establish Turkey as a modern state which looked to Europe as its model. At the time many names were in use for the city and the post office pleaded for a standardization of the name. Many Europeans had continued to use the old name of Constantinople and some used the abbreviated name "Stanboul" along with many Turks. The reason for the "b" is that many who speak Arabic and cognate languages find it difficult to pronounce the "p" and replace it with the sound of "b." (For those who have been in Israel, they may remember that the old city name for Caesarea Philippi was Paneas, the city of Pan, which has since become Banias.) The new name Istanbul caught on with Europeans and Turks quickly and the result was that it displaced the older names including the old Turkish name "Beyoglu' which is still used by some Turks today.

The City of Istanbul and the Ottomans. When Sultan **Mehmet II**, also known as *Fatih* ("the Conqueror") assumed the rule of the Ottomans in 1451, his goal was to capture the historic city. He immediately undertook the building of the *Rumeli Hisari* (a magnificent fortress on the European side of the Bosphous) and he repaired the earlier *Anadou Hisari* on the other side so that he was able to control the narrow straight. But the Byzantine defenders had closed the entrance to the Golden Horn with a great chain across the water which prevented the Ottoman ships from attacking the heart of the city from the north. During the night, however, Mehmet did what countless war strategists had done and continue to do. He used the night to execute his attack plan. Under cover of darkness he transported his boats overland and came up to the Golden Horn from the rear (like General Wolfe did later in the capture of Quebec City in Canada from the French). Mehmet quickly captured the major part of the city. The walls of the fortress, however, proved to be another matter until a Hungarian canon maker named Urban betrayed the Byzantines and supplied Mehmet with a huge canon that enabled the Ottomans to breach the walls. The **city fell on May 29, 1453** and effectively ended the shrunken Byzantine Empire.

[See Picture # 82 – The Third Court of the Topkapi Palace]

After his conquest, Mehmet set about to **emulate the building patterns** of the great Byzantine emperors like Constantine and Justinian with the construction of the **Topkapi Palace** north of the *Hagia Sophia* (now known as the Aya Sofya) on the picturesque promontory of the Golden Horn. This magnificent building, which once was the residence of the rich Ottoman sultans, is not only famed for its splendor but also for its harem as well as for its tales of intrigue and fascinating relationships which guides can share with you, if you are interested. Since the revolution, this palace is now a grand museum which houses some of the richest treasures in the world, such as the Spoonmakers's **Diamond** (86 carats) and the jeweled sword of Suleyman the Magnificent. But it also contains **religious treasures** such as hair that is reported to be from Mohamed and other items pertaining of the Muslim faith.

Like Mehmet, one of his successors, **Sultan Ahmet I** sought to prove his significance by building in the Sultanahmet area south of the Aya Sofya and near the ancient Hippodrome a mosque that would surpass the work of Justinian's building of the *Hagia Sophia*. The mosque, which was begun in 1606 and took ten years to build, is surrounded by six strategically placed minarets and a large courtyard that gives it a sense of grandeur. The interior is enhanced with thousands of Blue tiles which give the building a beautiful ambiance that has led it popularly to being called **"The Blue Mosque."** While the dome of the building is not as large or as grand as its earlier Justinian rival, it is a magnificent building which no one should miss in their visit to Istanbul.

[See Picture # 83 – The Blue Mosque]

The city is endowed with a number of great museums besides the Topkapi Palace and among them is the **Museum of Turkish and Islamic Art** which is housed in the former palace of Ibrahim Pasa, a confident of Suleyman the Magnificent but who fell out of favor with his patron and was strangled when others convinced the sultan that he was dangerous. The display of antique carpets is undoubtedly the best anywhere.

But for the person interested in **biblical history**, the most significant museum is the Istanbul **Archaeological Museum** which is housed in three separate buildings and which would take at least a day alone to visit. But I will try to provide a few highlights concerning these artifacts which have been removed from their places of origin by the Turkish conquerors. Even though the process was a little different than the way many western world museums have been stocked by purchasing artifacts that were pirated from their places of origin, the results are not much different.

In the Museum of Archeology are sarcophagi and mummies from Egypt and Sidon but perhaps the most noteworthy is the **marble sarcophagus** depicting *Alexander G*, although it was probably intended for Abdalonymos of Sidon. Also, here are a large statue *Alexander G*, a couple of altars to **gods unknown**, a stone **warning** gentiles not to enter the Jerusalem Temple, the early Gezer calendar and the famous inscription taken from the **water tunnel in Jerusalem** describing the meeting of both groups of diggers as they moved towards each other during the time of Hezekiah.

[See Picture # 84 – Museum Inscription from Hezekiah's Tunnel]
[in the Arcaeological Museum]

In the museum (Ancient Orient) are artifacts from the ancient city of Troy, a **relief** from the palace **Tiglath-Pileser III** of Assyria ("Pul" of the Bible) in Nimrud and another relief from **Sennacherrib's** palace in Nineveh showing slaves building his palace, sections from the **Ishtar Gate in Babylon**, and the historic **Kadesh Peace Treaty** between the Egyptians and the Hittites (1259 BC), a copy of which now hangs in the United Nations Security Council Chambers.

[See Pictures # 85 and # 86 – Artifacts from Ancient Babylon and Sumer]
[in the Istanbul Archaeology Museum]

Perhaps his most significant successor of Mehmet was **Suleyman the Magnificent** who was probably the richest of the Ottoman Sultans and was responsible for many of the significant buildings in the city. The most noteworthy of these buildings is the great mosque known as the **Suleymaniye** which was constructed on one of the most distinctive hills in Istanbul, a dominating structure in the entire area of the Golden Horn which lies just north of the Grand Bazar and the Istanbul University. Designed by Mimar Sinan, one of the greatest of the Muslim architects, the mosque is simply magnificent and it encompasses a number of services including a soup kitchen, a hospital and it has a popular restaurant which appeals to the nearby university students.

Among the popular sites for many visitors is the **Grand Bazar** which was initiated in the time of Mehmet and expanded steadily until it now covers a large triangular area of countless small shops and boutiques where bargaining for merchandise is expected. While various types of shops are interspersed throughout the Bazar, one can find some concentrations of fabric and copper in the north, carpets, jewelry and other ware in the mid section with gold products on the east side and leather products including suitcases and purses in south west, carpets in middle and more jewelry and leather in the southeast. Shopping and watching the activity in the Grand Bazar is a great treat for the visitor but be sure that you **protect your money, passport and valuables** because if they are lost there is little hope of recovery. And remember that **passports** are usually **only replaceable in Ankara**, not in Istanbul!

If you do not have the time to wander through the Grand Bazar, an alternative would be a brief

[See Picture # 87 – The Spice Bazar of Istanbul]

visit to the **Spice Bazar** where you can wander through the iron covered building and gain a sense of shopping in Istanbul. While there you will probably want to sample and take home some freshly made Turkish Delight or stock your kitchen with some rare spices.

[See Picture # 88 – The Majestic Fortress on the Bosphorus]

Finally, while much more could be said about this great city, one should not leave Istanbul without taking a **cruise on the Bosphorus** and viewing the city from the waterfront. I have taken the cruise a number of times and I have always enjoyed the experience, even during the time when I almost froze from the cold. But most of you who visit this great metropolis will do so when it is warm or even hot and you will bask in the sun as you pass on this brief voyage sights of countless mosques, fortress walls, palaces and great waterfront villas. It is an experience of relaxation in the midst of one of the busiest cities in the world where the traffic is almost always heavy.

C. TOUCHING WESTERN BITHYINIA

Chalcedon/Kadikoy: **(24)** Founded as early as the seventh century BC, the city of Chalcedon is the site of a double harbor but the currents in the Bosphorus made landing ships difficult and ultimately it gave way to the new city of Byzantium which had a much more amenable harbor situation (see above for the founding of Byzantium under Byzas and the tradition "Against the Blind").

Lying on the eastern (Asian) outskirts of Istanbul, not far from Nocomedia and north of Nicea is this famous town where the **Fourth Ecumenical Council** (AD 451) was held. In this city there had been located a significant Temple to Aphrodite which in the post-Constantinian period was refurbished and dedicated as a major Church to St. Euphemia who was martyred during the Diocletian persecution (303). This Church of St. Euphemia became the site of that Fourth Council that condemned Eutyches' view of the mixture of the two natures of Christ and set the stage for the historic approval of the **Chalcedonian Confession,** otherwise known as the **Nicene Creed** which is recited by many Christians today and clearly asserts that the human and divine natures of Jesus coexisted unmixed in one person.

Unfortunately, I can attest to the fact that for the Christian who is tracing the history of Christianity not much of the old city of Chalcedon remains while a visit to the site of Nicea is much more rewarding.

Nicomedia/Izmit: **(25)** Once Nicomedia was the major city of Bithynia and undoubtedly a goal of Paul's second missionary journey before he was summoned by a night vision to turn his focus of ministry to Macedonia (Acts 16:7-10). The city has suffered repeated earthquakes and sackings from both the north and the south. Today what remains of ancient Nicomedia is covered by the Turkish city of Izmit (a modern abbreviation for the ancient name).

The city lies at the eastern end of the narrow extension of the Sea of Marmara. It had what in ancient times could be regarded as a fine harbor and it was an important trade center for goods being transported between east and west. During the first century BC it became the capital of the Roman province of Bithynia and was made a center of Imperial worship in 29 BC. The city remained a strategic Roman city in Asia Minor and in the time of Diocletian it served as a major center for the persecution of Christians. In the modern world Istanbul has become the focal point of trade for the region.

Nicea/ Iznik: **(26)** Not far south from Istanbul, on the shore of Lake Iznik is the little out-of-the-way town of Nicea, known for its crafts and especially for tile-making (which was particularly significant during the 15th-17th centuries) but also for its important history, especially in the fourth century of our era. Founded by Antigonus, one of *Alexander's G* generals and named Antigonia in 316 BC, it was captured by his colleague Lysimachus fifteen years later in their dispute over territories and renamed for his wife, Nikaea. He fortified it with stout walls which were later enhanced with square towers during the first century AD. In the Roman period it sought to become the leading city of Bithynia but lost out to Nicomedia which had access to the Sea of Marmara and which became the capital of the province. Like much of Turkey, it has suffered from earthquakes and has been rebuilt a number of times with the help of emperors such as Vespasian, Trajan and Hadrian

Constantine built his **summer palace** here which became the sight of the **First Ecumenical Council** (AD 325) that condemned the teachings of Arius who sought to differentiate the **"essence"** of the Son (Jesus) from the Father. This Council began the multiple arguments that continued in later councils concerning the true nature of the Son and his relationship with the Father. Later, when Justinian was the emperor, he enhanced the city and refortified the walls and towers so that the city was able to survive the attacks of the Arabs but later succumbed to the invading Crusaders.

Of significance in visiting Nicea is the *Hagia Sophia* Church (Aya Sophia) which was the site of the **Seventh Ecumenical Council** (787) that legitimized the veneration of icons after the early iconoclastic controversy. The summer palace of Constantine often called the Palace of the Senate lies in ruins, mostly submerged in the nearby lake. The triangular Roman walls and the impressive gates provide a fascinating opportunity for picture-taking by the photographer. Also of significant interest a short distance from the city is the **Obelisk** of Cassius Philiskos which was constructed from five decreasing triangular-shaped stones on a large pedestal, while inside the city walls are the ruins of the Roman theater and the so-called **"Green Mosque"** (Yesil Cami) which was built by Sultan Murat I in the late fourteenth century. The Iznik Museum contains some significant statuary from the past as well as fine examples of its well-known tiles.

D. MOVING SOUTH THROUGH ANCIENT MYSIA

In the trek south to reach the cities of the Book of Revelation (Apocalypse of John) a traveler may choose to go south from Istanbul and through western Bithyinia to Nicea in order to reach Bursa and Balikesir and then south to Thyatira/Akhisar (which is the plan I am following in this book). Alternatively, one may travel west from Istanbul on the northern (European) side of the Sea of Marmara and cross the Dardanelles by ferry to the Asian side near Canakkala. Thereafter, one would head south past Truva (ancient Troy) and on to Purgamum/Bergama. I have also followed this latter route but for the purposes of this book, I am using a reverse plan ultimately to reach the borders of Thrace or Greece and continue to Alexandropolis and Phiippi.

Bursa/Prusa: **(27)** Today Bursa is lovely center with parks running throughout its environs and clearly one of the major cities of Turkey with a population of about **two million** people. It was the **first capital of the Ottoman Empire** and it still displays some memory of the opulence that once was present in this place. During its early history it was subject to the power and authority of Purgamum when Eumenes II seized it, but it passed into Roman control when Attalus III at his death bequeathed the kingdom to Rome (133 BC). In the early Byzantine period the city became an important vacation and recreation center when the thermal baths in the area (at Cekirge) were developed and the city was enhanced significantly by Justinian.

About five hundred years later began a time of turmoil for the city and the region. During that period of wars between the Muslims and the Crusaders the city was conquered repeatedly by opposing forces and it finally fell into Ottoman hands when **Osman Gazi** (the son of Ertugrul) finally took the city in 1326 and established it as the capital of the newly forming Ottoman Empire. His successor, **Orhan Gazi** adopted the title of **"Sultan"** and set the goal for his successors to conquer Constantinople/Byzantium which feat was finally accomplished by Mehmet II in 1453 (see the discussion above). But the days of Bursa as the capital the Ottoman empire were numbered because in order to prepare for the control of the entire region, the conquest of Constantinople and the assault on Europe, the Ottomans moved their capital in 1403 to the north and the old capital of the Roman province of Thrace which was **Hadrianopolis** later merely designated as Adrianopolis and which today is known as **Edirne** near the boader with Greece and Bulgaria.

Among the important sites to visit in Bursa is the "Green Mosque" (Yesil Cami) constructed by Mehmet I in the third decade of the fifteenth century. In distinction from its earlier counterpart in Nicea built by Murat I which followed the Persian model brought to Turkey by the Seljuks, this mosque represents an innovation in the building pattern with beautiful marble facades and the use of tiles that give a soft colored ambiance to the building that is recognizable throughout Turkey.

Also significant in visiting the city to the west is the area known as Muradiye with a mosque which follows the pattern of Yesil Cami and a cemetery in which some significant Ottoman leaders have been buried, including the rather simple tomb of Murat II who verged on being an ascetic and reigned for about thirty years. South and east of Muradiye is the area of the Citadel or Hisar (fortress) with its stone walls and a park that contains the tombs of the two early Gazi leaders, Osman and Orhan, who established the Ottoman Dynasty. Nearby is the lofty clock tower which is reminder of the magnificent buildings that once stood in this grand old city which has suffered from several earthquakes. To the east of the Citadel is the Ulu Cami Mosque which is one of the most striking buildings in Bursa (with its twenty domes) that was built at the end of the fourteenth century as a modified answer to a pledge made by Yildirim Beyazit in return for his victory over the Crusaders.

Finally, one should not miss the opportunities in Bursa of shopping for silk products in this center of the silk industry or of tasting the Bursa "kebap."

Balikesir: **(28)** Coming from Istanbul and the northeast, Balikesir serves as convenient overnight place to rest before heading south to Thyatira/Akhisar and visiting the cities mentioned in the Book of Revelation. From this point on can choose to travel southwest Pergamum or directly south Thyatira.

D. CIRCLING AROUND THE CHURCHES OF REVELATION

1. PART I – THE FIRST THREE CHURCHES

Thyatira/Akhisar: **(29)** Situated in a great plain approximately 50 miles (80 km) northeast of Smyrna (Izmir) near the Lycus River, the city was an important intersection between Sardis to the south and Peragmum to the northwest. Its location and lack of natural defenses explains why it was rather easily conquered and exchanged hands between Selucids (from Syria) and the Attalids (from Pegamum) as well as the Bythinians under Prusias. It came under Roman control when Attalus III bequeathed his Peragaminian kingdom to Rome in 133 BC. Habitation of the city from archaeological evidence seems to date back to sometime around the beginning of the third millennium BC but it is difficult to gain extensive confirmation of its development because the modern city of Akhisar with over 80,000 people living around the site makes extensive investigation of the site at least for the present virtually impossible. Nevertheless, part of the ancient acropolis of the city has been uncovered since it is the area where the hospital park and garden are located. The early Lydian name "Teira" probably means "town" or "walled city."

During the Roman period Thyatira was very prosperous and there was a great influx of people from regions to east and south, including Phyrgians, other Lydians and even Galatians. Inscriptions found in the area validate the fact that the Roman city contained many guilds including various metal workers such as blacksmiths and copper craftsmen, textile labors and merchants, dyers, and leather workers. These guilds had special gods that they honored and guild meals normally were conducted as dedicated feasts to theses gods, which can explain the warning to Thyatira in Revelation 2:20 concerning eating food sacrificed to idols. The dying industry was especially noteworthy here because of the rich purple and dark red colors which came from shell fish and other sources that were available in this area and were widely desired among the ancients throughout the Mediterranean basin. The influx of people from the east into this prosperous area during this period also explains the story in Acts 16:14-15 of Paul's meeting in Philippi with Lydia (or the Lydian woman) who was a merchant of purple dye doing business in Macedonia.

Syncretism was a common reality during this time in Thyatira and the rest of the province of Asia and while the most revered god in Thyatira was Apollo, he had a host of other names including Pythius and Tyrimnaeus which represented the mixture of cultures that was present in that place. At the heart of the critique of the church in Thyatira in the Apocalypse is syncretism and Jezebel who forced Baal, Asherah and other worship on Israel became for John an historic symbol of syncretistic worship (1 Kgs 16:31; 21:25-26).

Among the historic buildings that can be seen in Thyatira/Akhisar is the great mosque (Ulu Cami) which has been converted several times during its existence. It was first a Roman temple, then it apparently served as some sort of political center, thereafter it seems to have been used as a Byzantine church and at present it is the oldest mosque in the city. Guides may mention the fact that one inscription that has been found confirms the presence of Jews in the city and refers to the synagogue as a *sabbateion* (Sabbath house). While a synagogue is not mentioned in the letter to Thyatira, John was aware of the presence of Jews in this area from the fact that mention is made of a "synagogue of Satan" in connection with the letters to Smyrna and Philadelphia (Rev 2:9; 3:9).

Smyrna/Izmir: (30)

Izmir is today Turkey's third largest city boasting a population of nearly three million people. As one strides along the waterfront especially at sunset, the visitor can gain the feeling of a place where one can enjoy being on a vacation. The people in Izmir tend to be more oriented to European patterns than in most of the other places in Turkey with the exception of its larger sister city on the Bosphorus and it is regarded by many Turks as the most liberal, educated city in Turkey.

Although Smyrna was probably founded around 1000 BC on the waterfront by Aeolian settlers from Greece, it struggled to gain the importance it should have had since it had a significant harbor on a strategic protected bay (Izmir) just off the Aegean Sea. But it lacked a defensible setting and

succumbed to onslaughts from others who wanted to control the area such as: the Ionians who drove out the Aeolians in the eighth century and the Lydians who sacked the city and left it in ruins at the end of the seventh century. According to a questionable story, *Alexander G* is reputed to have had a vision to **reestablished the city** on the slope of Mt. Pagus but it was probably his feuding successors Antigonus and Lysimachus who reestablished Smyrna on the more defensible site of the side of the mountain.

When Smyrna came into Roman hands, it was quickly recognized as a strategic port city. It soon gained prominence, taking its position as a special imperial city along side of the more established cities of Ephesus and Pergamum and gaining favor with Roman authorities who granted Smyrna the right to construct (195 BC) the first **temple to *Dea Roma*** in the entire region. But when it aligned itself with Mithridates VI of Pontus who revolted against Rome and slaughtered 80,000 Roman citizens during the first third of the first century BC, Smyrna lost its favored status. Then after murdering Julius Caesar in 43 BC Brutus and Cassius assembled their forces in Smyrna before meeting Antony, Octavian and Lepidus in the historic battle of Philippi.

Among the important figures associated with Smyrna one can probably count Homer who it has been argued was a native of Meles, which is a local river in that area. A stellar Christian figure associated with Smyrna is Polycarp, the well-known bishop of Smyrna who at the age of 86 in AD 156 was burned at the stake in the stadium of Smyrna because he refused to give up his faith in Jesus. According to Irenaeus, his student, Polycarp had studied personally with the evangelist John and had heard the gospel recounted from other disciples of Jesus[12]. In his reported final speech in which he boldly proclaimed continuing loyalty to Christ after "eighty-six years" he undoubtedly recalled that earlier Ignatius, the bishop of Syrian Antioch, had stopped in Smyrna on his way to his execution in Rome (c. 107) and had written a letter of encouragement to him and the church at Smyrna. The Catholic Church dedicated to the memory of St. Polycarp is the oldest church in Smyrna. But Polycarp was not the only martyr there. Eusebius (*H.E.* iv. 15f.) details other martyrs such as Germanicus who was killed by wild animals or some who were burned at the stake.

While Izmir is a thriving city, a few areas have been excavated such as the central forum which was reconstructed by Marcus Aurelius after the great earthquake in 178 and Turkish authorities have slowly been acquiring strategic additional properties in order to authorized continuing archaeological work in the city. Among the interesting sites to visit are the reconstructed section of the magnificent colonnaded way in the forum and the head and shoulders portrait of Faustina, the wife of Aurelius, which has been etched into one of the stone arches in the west colonnade. This forum area served as the civic, judicial and state center for the city. While we know that an altar to Zeus was a central feature of the forum, remains of this altar are missing. Among the significant discoveries from ancient Smyrrna is the Temple of Athena built as early the seventh century BC and although it was damaged and rebuilt several times a major part has been restored which provides us with some insight into what the beautiful shrine must have been like. Vestiges of the aquaduct system that supplied water to this important city are also still evident.

---

[12] See the Latin Letter with an English translation written by Irenaeus to Florinius (a Roman presbyter) c. AD 190 in Daniel J. Theron, *Evidence of Tradition* (Grand Rapids: Baker Book House,1958), 24-27.

Reliefs taken from the forum, now housed in the **Izmir Archaeological Museum,** depict the gods of the pantheon such as Artemis (a favorite of the Asians) and Demeter (the caring protectress of agriculture) who are often pictured together and here with Poseidon/Neptune (the Sea god) who was clearly important to a harbor city like Smyrna. Also in the museum are various "inscriptions" both originally intended and later graffiti, of which some have a Christian origin. Overlooking the city on Mt. Pagus is the area of the **Kadifekale**, the "velvet fortress," the foundations for the walls of which go back to the time of Lysimachus. As one might expect, this acropolis area has been the focus of attacks on the city and therefore has been repeatedly refortified and strengthened. The area was commonly referred to as the "crown" of the city (cf. Rev 2:10 where John employs the idea of "crown of life" as the secure expectation of faithful Christians).

Ephesus and its Environs: **(14, 21 and 22)** South of Izmir lies the historic area of Ephesus (14, 22), the leading city in the Roman Province of Asia. For a detailed discussion of Ephesus as well as Kusadasi (21) and Selcuk/Ayaseluk (22) see section A of this chapter.

2. THREE NEARBY SITES

I now pause to review two cities which are not directly associated with the seven churches of Revelation and may not be on some organized tours of the area but which can generally be attached to our study of Paul. They are Miletus and its smaller sister city of Priene.

Also, before rejoining the seven cities, I am here adding a brief discussion on Aphrodisias for completeness because it is one of the great archaeological sites along the way in Western Turkey before reaching town of Laodicea.

Priene/Gullubahce and Miletus/Milet/Balat: South of Ephesus on the way to the major city of Miletus is the small model town of Priene which requires a brief statement.

Priene/Gullubahce: **(31)** Priene was probably founded before the tenth century BC but almost nothing remains from that era since it suffered several destructions at the hands of the Persians and ultimately required a **complete rebuilding** around 350 BC. The city is perched high on the slope of Mt. Mykale and it was constructed according to a sophisticated grid plan which was unique for the time. Among the most significant remains in this ancient city is **the Temple of Athena** which was designed by **Pythius**, the renowned architect who was responsible for the famous mausoleum of Halicarnassus that some scholars regard as one of the wonders of the ancient world. This Temp;le of Athena became a model for other builders to copy because it is considered by many as perhaps the finest of the Ionian temples built. While most of the columns have fallen, five have been reerected by archaeologists in order to provide the visitor with a sense of what the original bulding must have been like.

While the new city was never intended to have a population of much more than 5,000 residents, near the Temple of Athena is a magnificent **theater** (perhaps the best preserved in the entire region) which seated approximately 6,500 with elaborate seats for special guests. The **bouleterion** (council chamber) which was located southeast of the theater is likewise a fine example of refined architecture. Of special note on the edge of the town was the discovery of the **synagogue,** one of the few found in the region. It had been a private home that was renovated and archaeologists discovered several menorah wall plaques and a niche in the eastern wall for the scrolls. Also here, just south of both the Athena temple and the theater there was found a **Byzantine church** and south of it was the city's **agora** with an altar and shrine to Zeus. On the far west near the cliff and overlooking the sea is a building known s the **Alexandrium** where *Alexander G* is reputed to have resided during his siege of Miletus. Similar to practices in our world, the place where he stayed then apparently became a shrine to the famous general containing a stature of the warrior and perhaps some other memorabilia.

While the city is not mentioned in the Bible, the early Chritians must have been quite aware of the presence of this important town. Moreover, the **Ephesian elders** would most likely have passed very close to it on the road as they made their jouney from Ephesus to meet Paul in Miletus (Acts 20:17-22) when he was on his way to Jerusalem prior to his arrest and his trip to Rome as a prisoner.

Miletus/Milet/Balet: **(32)** Miletus of Antiquity was a major **commercial and naval center** having four strategic harbors which were natural coves that were carved out of a rather slim penninsula which jutted into the southern part of the **Latmus Gulf**. To make it even more ideal for shipping, it was also protected from most heavy seas of the Aegean and Mediterranean by the island of Lade. Because of its strategic location, lying about 14 miles (22 km) south of Priene, Miletus which was a Mycenaen settlement was already a significant city by the beginning of the first millennium BC. Its **trade routes** stretched to the west as far as Egypt, to the north and the Black Sea and to the east as far as the shores of Mesopotamia and beyond. It prospered as an economic hub for Asia Minor.

But its easy acess to the sea also meant that it was vulnerable to powerful naval forces like **Persia** which gained control of the city in 546 BC. When the citizens of Miletus resited the captors, their ships were destroyed in the Battle of Lade and the city was then reduced to rubble in 494. The positive aspect of this destruction, however, was that in the rebuilding phase, like its smaller neighbor Priene across the gulf, the city was laid out very carefully according to the Hippodamian square grid plan and the result was the development of a superbly designed city.

Alexander G breathed new life into the city with his historic victories over the Persians and by freeing Miletus from the periodic clutches of its Persian nemisis in 334 BC. After Alexander's death Lysimachus, one of his generals, became a strong supporter of the city which led to a period of great prosperity for the city. The **Romans** took control of the region in 133 BC and imposed and exorbinate tax burden on the people that within four years led to a powerful uprising against Rome. The result was that thousands of Roman supporters were brutally killed. While the Romans regained control of the situation, during this period there was great turmoil in Rome and it did not handle its subject people well which led to a further uprising forty years later with Mithradates of Pontus that spread throughout Asia and led to thousands of Romans again being slaughtered.

Once stability was reasserted in Rome, especially with Augustus, then the situation imporoved throughout the newly formulated Empire and Miletus once again prospered. But its days were numbered, not because of enemies but because of the **Menander River** and its pattern of carrying silt to the sea. Just like the situation in Ephesus and the silting of the Cayster River which closed the great harbor there so that city became removed from the water and was no longer a seaport, so today the entire area around Miletus is rather swampy and the old harbors are no longer open or viable. While the population of the city probably did not reach 100,000, the area of ancient Miteus is sizable but beyond the center is not too easy to negotiate because of the marsh lands.

Yet visiting the ruins of this ancient city and reflecting on its past is still a significant experience. Especially memorable is overlooking the Harbor from the theater which once had a cauldric statute that perhaps represented the Mediterranean basin and was originally dedicated Pompey for his far-reachng exploits but later was assigned to Augustus since Pompey fell out of favor with Caesar. Unforgettable will be the experience of climbing the steps of the **magnificent theater** which overlooks the Theater Harbor. It originally seated 15,000 but was expanded to approximately 25,000 in Roman times, although some of the upper seating is now missing. At its peak the large stage must have seemed breath-taking, reaching a height of three stories so that those attending woul have been given the feeling of grandure with the front row containing a specially designed royal box marked by pillars for the emperor and his guests. Interestingly, one section is marked for "the **Jews** (*eioudeon*) who are also 'Godfearers' (*theosebeon*)" or "Jews and Godfearers." The meaning is not exactly clear but the presence of Jews in the theater along with other special groups is quite clear and is in direct contrast to some of the strictures which were promulgated by rabbis in Israel. I make this special point here becsue some people have challenged my view of the Apoclypse (**Boodk of Revelaion**) as a theatrical drama by arguing that Jews did not attend pagan theaters and would not understand the theater.[13]

To the near north of the theater the Byzantines constructed their **fortress** and beyond the fortress lies the **Lion Harbor** that originally had two great lion statues which welcomed ships coming into port much like the Merlion stands on the shore of the central bay as a symbol of **Singapore**. Overlooking this harbor stands the ruins of the central Temple to **Apollo Delphinios** which was the patron god of the seafaring Miletians and represented the merging of Apollo with the Dolphin god much like the Merlion is a merging of a lion and a mermaid. This temple was constructed with an open court surrounded by porches or stoa and was apparently built around 6th century BC although the worship of Apollo probably was initiated earlier with the arrival of seafaring Ionian immigrants from the mainland of Greece.

Running south of the Delphinion, as it is normally called, are the remains of two forums or agoras between which was the bouleutarion (city council chamber). South of the Delphinion and running

---

[13] See Gerald Borchert "The Book of Revelation" in *NLT Study Bible* (Carol Stream, IL, Tyndale house Publishers, 2008), especially at 2172-78.

along the east side of the northern and south agoras was the great **Sacred or Processional Way** which stretched some 14 miles (23 km) from this temple in Miletus to the giant **Temple of Apollo in Didyma** which was constructed with **122 columns, second only in size** to the Temple of Atemis in Ephesus with its 127 columns. Incorporated into the beginning of this Processional Way was a gigantic **Nymphaeum** or fountain together with a shrine to the god Asclepius which later was destroyed and a Byzanitine chuch replace it. Finally, among the many other structures that once graced the city of Miletus mention should be made of the fact that to the west of the south agora and overlooking the Theater Harbor, **Faustina** (the wife of Marcus Aurelius) built a large **Bath House** and to the south of the theater harbor, the stadium and western agora stands the remains of the early Temple to Athena which was built at the beginning of the fifth century BC.

Among the **significant names** of non-military and non-political figures that have been associated with Miletus I pause to mention only a few. One cannot avoid noting that Thales, Anaximander and Anaximenes who were citizens of Miletus. Thales has been regarded by many as one of the "seven early sages" which included Bias and Solon. Thales, Anaximander and Anaximenes, according to Windelband, were all from the Melesian school of Natural Philosophy which wrestled with the original ground of things and their relationship to the nature of change.[14] Isodorus was one of the architects for Hagia Sophia in Constantiople

Miletus is mentioned several times in **the Bible**, primarily in reference to the conclusion of Paul's third journey as he was on his way to Jerusalem where he would be arrested. Rather than stopping in Ephesus on this journey, he summoned the **Ephesian elders** to come to Miletus for a final meeting with him in which he passionately told them of his divine calling to go to Jerusalem and that their duty was to take care of their charges as Christian leaders because difficult times were coming and false teachers would be divisive and would tear apart their congregations (Acts 20:15-38). The city is also mentioned in 2 Timothy 20 in reference to Paul leaving the sick **Trophimus** (a Gentile follower) in Miletus. Unfortunately, it is difficult to fit this reference into Luke's account of Paul's journeys and only speculation is possible. The only other mention of Miletus is a passing reference to "wool from Miletus" (*miletou*) in **Ezekiel** 27:18 of the Septuagint (the Greek of the OldTestament). The city is not mentioned in the Hebrew text.

Aphrodisias/ Afrodisias/Geyre: **(33)** It would be hard not to rate Aphrodisias as one of great archaeological sites in Turkey, a site which consumed the attention of archaeologist **Kenan Erin** of New York University who is buried in a beautiful plot near the excellent little **museum** that has been opened to honor his and others superb findings from the site. Yet because the site is not mentioned in the Bible, the entire place is skipped by most visitors who travel to the tri-cities of Laodicea, Hierapolis and Colossae. I add it here because it provides such a **marvelous example of an ancient Hellenistic city** without confronting the bustling crowds one finds at the renowned larger site of Ephesus.

[See Picture # 89 – The Theater and Civic Agora at Aphrodisias]

---

[14] See Wilhelm Windelband, *A History of Philosophy*, Vol. I (New York; Harper and Brothers, 1901), 27.

In a fairly confinced area one can find a fine example of a ancient **theater** which may have seated as many as 10,000 people, an excellent example of an **odeon** for music performances and lectures which would have seated more than 1500 listeners, and a large, magnificent **hippodrome/stadium** (about 875 ft./270 m. long) which would have accommodated a huge crowd of about 30,000 spectators. During the height of the gladiatorial games the eastern end of the hippodrome was converted into an area for gladiatorial games (see the picture). Also present here are a well-preserved **bouletarion** (council chamber), a civic agora, bath houses and a temple to Rome (Dea Roma) and the deified caesars. The visitor may wonder how a place like Aphrodisias, which may seem to be nowhere important, could have been so significant and attracted such crowds. But it must be remembered that area contexts change over time.

[See Picture # 90 – A Section of the 30,000 seat Hippodrome at Aphrodisias]

A brief review of the site and the ancient mound indicates that the site was probably settled as early as the fifth millennium BC although not much remains from the earliest periods. Most of the major buildings that have been uncovered date from the Hellenistic era sometime after the third century BC and that it probably reached its zenith around the third century AD when it became the **capital** of the late Roman province of **Caria** and certainly by that point probably reached a population size of between fourteen and eighteen thousand.

[See Picture # 91 – Ruins of the Temple of Aphrodite at Aphrodisias]

The ancient focus for worship and pilgrimages here, as one might suspect, was to the **Temple of Aphrodite**, the earliest vestiges of her shrine probably date back to the sixth century BC. The remains of the larger Temple which we can see is probably from about the third century BC and the building indicates that it was transformed into a Christian Church around the middle of the fifth century AD. Part of the temple has been restored by archaeologists and a frieze of the **frolicking virgin goddess** is in the museum.

[See Picture # 92 – Frieze of Aphrodite in the Museum of Aphrodisias]

3. PART II – THE LAST FOUR CHURCHES

The Tri-cities of Laodicea, Colossae and Hierapolis

Laodicea: **(34)** If you read the seventh letter of Revelation, you might ask: "Who would want to be from Laodicea?" Yet the statement that you are "neither cold nor hot.... [but] lukewarm" (Rev 3:15) reflects an important historical reality concerning **the water** in the area of the tri-cities. Laodicea's lime filled water came came from the Baspinar Springs about 8 km (5 miles) away and could be contrasted to both Hierapolis (c. 5 ½ mi./9 km) with its very warm calcium loaded spring water and Colossae (c. 10 miles) with its considerabley better water.[15] In viewing the richness of the people and the apparent lack of authentic Christian living among some believers in the church of Laodicea, John used **vivid imagery** in the Book of **Revelation** to provide a picture of God's sickening reaction to pseudo-commitment on the part of followers of Jesus.

According to the senior **Pliny**, Laodicea was established on the site of an early settlement named Diospolis (the city of Zeus, chief of the gods) who became the patron god of the city (cf. Pliny, *Natual History* v.105). In its later existence the city was founded by the Seleucid king **Antiochus II** and was named for his first wife **Laodice**. Following the **defeat of Antiochus III** (the so-called "Great") by the combined forces of the Romans and the Pergamenes at the Battle of Magnesia (189 BC), the Treaty of Apamea the next year allowed the Attulids of Pergamum to gained control of the city until Attulus III bequesthed his kingdom to Rome on his death (133 BC). Then in 129 Rome created the **new province of Asia** from much of the former Pergamese kingdom. In the great **uprising** of the Asians against Rome under **Mithradates** of Pontus during the eighties when tens of thousands of Romans were slaughtered, the Laodiceans sensed the folly of such a rebellion and were one of only a handful of cities that **refused** to side with the other Asians. Sensing the need rewin the loyalties of Asia, Rome in 26 BC issued the offer of allowing the building of a second imperial temple to Dea Roma in Asia (besides Pergamum). The Laodiecean bid was rejected for lack of adequate funding in favor of Smyrna which had been on the other side. Ultimately Laodicea did erect imperial temples in honor of Commodus and Caracalla although those choices were hardly the most commendable and the names of both were the subjects of rejection.

Whatever may have been the truth concerning the **economic condition** of Laodicea during the earlier period, it is very clear that Laodicea did not continue to be impoverished into the first century AD because when the **great earthquake of AD 60** occurred that devastated many cities in that area, Laodicea declined the need for assistance from Rome and as **Tacitus** records, it "recovered from its own resources, apart from our assistance" (*Annals* xiv.27). There is little doubt that by the middle of the first century AD Laodicea was a **wealthy banking center**, confirming the prideful economic evaluation of it in Revelation 3:17.

In addition, the reference to the need for white garments noted in verse 18 fits the fact that Laodicea had a prosperous textile industry and that text contrasts vividly with the highly desirable **soft, raven black wool** that was produced in the city and in fact was used in the manufacture of popular Roman tunics. The additional reference reference to the need for **"eye salve"** or "ointment" in verse 18 can certainly be said to reflect John's recognition that there was a medical center in the city. Whether he was aware that the school produced early opthamologists like **Demosthes Philalethes**, he apparently understood that some topical ointment such as Phygian eye powder was produced there since zinc and alum were available in that area and traded in the markets there (cf. Strabo, *Geographica* xii.8.19-20).

---

[15] I should add a note here similar to that of Mark Wilson who reminds us of the frequent misconception among Christians that the sulfer water of Hierapolis not drinking water and was never transported by aquaduct to Laodicea (see his *Biblical Turkey: A Guide to the Jewish and Christian Sites of Asia Minor* [Istanbul; Yayinlari, 2010], 253).

The presence of a large **Jewish population** is confirmed by the fact that the somewhat illustrious Flaccus who was serving as proconsul for that area in AD 62 seized approximately twenty Roman pounds of **gold** that was headed for the Jerusalem Temple from the annual half shekel collection on the basis that the exporting of gold was ruled illegal and the relations of Rome with Jerusalem was tenuous at best during that time (Cicero, *Pro Flacco*, 68).

Besides the references to Laodicea in the Book of Revelation, one should mention the the fact that the city is mentioned in Colossians 2:1 where **Paul**[16] expresses his concrn for the Chrisitans in both Colossae and Laodicea. There he also clearly asserts that they have "not seen my face." This statement probably means that **Epaphras,** from whom Paul learned about their situation, was probably the founder of the churches in the Lycus Valley (cf. Col 1:7).

[See Picture # 93 - The Laodicean Temple of Artemis was changed into a church]

Moreover, in the closing greetings of the **Colossian letter** Paul ties Laodicea to Hierapolis as well by indicating that Epaphras was a hardworking leader in both churches (Col 4:13) and he mentions that the church of Laodicea met in the home of **Nympha** indicating here as elsewhere in the Pauline epistles the important role that women played in the leadership of the early churches (4:15). Finally, in verse 16 Paul charges the Colossians to read his **letter to Laodicea** and have the Laodiceans read his Colossian letter. Of course, questions are bound to rise in the minds of readers because we do not have a letter to Laodicea. Some scholars have suggested that Ephesians was this letter since we know that copies of this epistle circulated without "in/at Ephesus" (*en epheso*, Eph 1:1). Whether or not that suggestion is a correct conclusion remains a **speculation** because at present we do not have sufficient information to make a confirmed judgment.

Visiting the site of Laodicea is an experience of seeing a **work in process**. Not long ago visitors could see two theaters, the outline of both a stadium and a forum as well as the ruins of a basilica and stones strewn everywhere. But the situation is changing as archeaologists are at work piecimg stones together and uncovering other remains. Indeed, as they continue to dig, they have left some stones *in situ* below the surface and covered the area with plexiglass so that people can see the way they had been lying under the earth.

Summarizing some facts which we know, Laodicea was basically oriented to the Hippodamian **grid plan** with its **main road** running from the west (the Ephesian Gate) to the the east (the Syrian Gate). The names of the gates should provide readers with an indication of the fact that the city is on the main east-west highway transversing Asia Minor from Ephesus and the sea on the west to Tarsus and Mesopotamia on the east. About a third of the way into the city from the Ephesian Gate the road crosses a smaller road running north to the Hierapoltian Gate and south to the Aphrodisian Gate.

[See Picture # 94 - Partly Reconstructed Temple and the Central Agora of Laodicea]

---

[16] I am not here intending to join the scholarly debate about who wrote Colossians. I have expressed my view on Paul's authorship of this book in Gerald L. Borchert, *Worship in the New Testament: Divine Mystery and Human Response* (St. Louis: Chalice Press, 2008), 147.

Approximately at the midpoint of the main Laodicean city road there is a jog where one encounters the remains of another north-south road along which was a large fountain (nymphaeum) dedicated to Caracalla and the remains of a colonnaded street. Near the crossing point was the main bath house, the remains of a temple, a nymphaeum built to honor Septimus Servus and nearby is the central forum/agora, while to east of of this complex archaeologists have recently uncovered what appears to have been a baptisry. To the far south was a complex containing the bouletarion (council chamber), civic forum, gymnasium and bath house with a water reservoir and south of it was a large stadium.

[See Picture # 95 – Remains of the Western Theater of Laodicea]

To the far north are the **two theaters**, the west (smaller) one was probably built in the second century BC with a seating capacity of bout 8,000 and even though it was expanded, it apparently did not suffice so a larger one was built to the east in the second century AD facing more to the north and seating at least 12,000. These theaters continued in use beyond the time of Justinian but after the city was abandoned because of the great **earthquake** at the beginning of the **seventh century**, the stones of the theatres were repeatedly scavenged for use in buildings of nearby towns. To the west of the northern jog in the main road are the remains of a fairly substantial Byzantine church. Finally, as one walks among the ruins, archaeologists have revealed that the visitor repeatedly crosses over a well-constructed ancient **drainage and sewer system** and one can also discover an elaborate system of ceramic and clay **pipes** that that carried **water** from the Baspinar Springs to the homes and public buildings of the city, many of which are greatly encrusted with lime indicating the poor quality of the water there.

Colossae/Honaz: **(35)** Located about 16 km (10 miles) from Laodicea on the bank of the Meader, a tributary of the Lycus River, it was positioned near the base of Mt Cadmus/Honaz and the aquifer which provided the souce for its better **water** than Laodicea and Hierapolis. As early as the fifth century BC, according to **Heroditus** (*Historiae* vii.30), Colossae was reguarded as **the bustling, important city** in the area. Later the city shrunk in importance as Hierapolis and Laodicea emerged as the strategic cities near the crossroads of the trans-Asian highway and the northwest highway from Pergamum. The ancient site is about 12 miles (19 km) from the modern city of Denizli with its population of about a half million people and about 120 miles (nearly 200 km) east of ancient Ephesus and the sea coast.

Like other cities in the area, it was renowned for its textile industry and particularly Colossae was known for its expesive purple-reddish wool. Also, like its neighbors the city was devastated by **earthquakes** which necessitated periodic rebuilding. After the traumatic upheaval in AD 60 it continued as a smaller center but it never fully recovered its earlier vitality. The city site was completely abandoned in the late Byzantine period and today what remains is an **unexcavated mound** (*hoyuk*) marked by a few stones and outlines of some earlier bildings which attract very few visitors.

An **important letter** was addressed to the chuch at Colossae by the Pauline company (Paul and Timothy as well Tychicus and Onesimus; cf. Col 1:1; 4:7, 9) concerning the significance of Christ (Col 1:15-20) and the importance of baptism as a key to living the Christian life (3:1-2, 5, 8, 12, etc). **Paul** is not mentioned in the Bible as having visited this city (see 2:1). Instead, he apparently learned of the situation in the church from **Apaphras** whom we surmise was the founder of the churches in the Lycus Valley (cf. 1:7). An interesting note in Colossians 4:7-9 ties this letter directly with the short letter to **Philemon** through the runaway slave **Onesimus** whom Paul led to Christ and ultimately sent back to his owner with the firm advice to treat Onesimus as a brother (Phlm 16). Philemon together with his wife Apphia are noted as being the sponsors of a churh here and the mention of a colleague Archippus as a "a fellow soldier" (v. 2) together with Paul designating himself as an "ambassador" (v.9) are **suggestive** that Philemon may have been a signifiaant government **official** in the city.

Hierapolis/Pamukkale: (36)

The third of the ancient tri-cities Hierapolis remains important today as a **popular tourist center** because of its unusal formation of **white calicified travertine cliffs** that can be seen from a fair distance. These calcifed forms provide an explanation for its modern name of Pamukkale or "cotton castle." Visiting the site is a delightful experience which provides the combination of encountering a picturesque **natural physical phenomenon** created by the hot water that bubbles forth from the earth along with the popular bath houses and swimming pools that were constructed in the context of a well developed **archaeological site** which was made more interesting with the recently discovered tomb of the Apostle Philip and a wonderful little **museum** which provides helpful information concerning the history of Hierapolis.

[See Picture # 96 – The Famous White Calcified Cliffs of Hierapolis –]
[Pamukkale ("Cotton Castle")]

Like the other tri-cities, it lies near the large modern city of Denizli and is in an area subject to earthquakes which has necessitated periodic rebuilding of some of the structures. The time of its actual founding is a little shrouded. It is clear that it was part of the area that came under the control of the Pergamese king **Eumenes II after the Treaty of Apama** which passed Phyrgian and Lydian territories of the Seleucids into the the hands of the Attalid family for their support of Rome in 188 BC. But it was likely founded earlier by the Seuecids when Antiochus III was stretching his authority and settled displaced Jews in the region. A number of tombs in the **necropolis** (ancient grave yard) are replete with carvings of the **menorah** on them, indicating the early presence of Jews in the city.

The source of the name "Hierapolis" is also a little in question. Popularly it is known as the **"Holy City"** (from the Greek *heira polis*) which would fit the fact that it had a number of temples in it. But the name may also be derived from **"Hiera,"** the wife of Telephus, the grandson of Zeus and the son of Hercules, who was the so-called mythical founder of Pergamum.[17] As with the other cities of

---

[17] While the ancient myths are not all consistent, Zeus fathered Hercules (one of the great heros of Greek mythology) by Princess Alcmene. Hera, the wifeof Zeus, was always frustrated by the existence of Hercules and

the region, the territory was bequeathed to Rome at the death of Attulus III in 133 BC and became part of the province of Asia in 129 BC.

The patron god of the city was **Apollo**, the ruins of whose temple are still visible and even though this temple was probably from the time of Caracalla or Geta, it was probably built on the site of the former Hellenistic temple. **Similar to Delphi**, the temple was regarded as sacrosanct and was the seat of a famous **oracle**. As one might guess, the **vaporous gasses** which bubbled out with the mineral water from below the surface were regarded as sacred and a **Plutonium** was established in a cave near the temple which was associated with Pluto/Hades, the god of the underworld. Entrance to the cave is blocked today so that visitors will not be tempted to breath the poisonous gases which used to be employed by the sacred priests to **prove the toxic nature** of the gases by thrusting small birds and animals into the outlets in the earth while claiming priestly invulnerability. It is intruging to remember that the lord/king of this underground chamber was also known as "**Apollyon**," the destroyer, (note the close relation to the name of Apollo) who is mentioned in **Revelation 9:11** as the angel of the bottomless pit.

Not far from the temple complex is a magnificent **Roman Theater** initiated by Hadrian and expanded by Septimius Severus which at its peak would have seated at least 12,000 people. Further to the west is an earlier Hellenistic theater which lies in ruins. Near the earlier theater is the giant **Agora/Forum** which once must have been spectacular since it was enclosed on three sides with beautiful marble porticos unlike many of the other buildings in Hierapolis which are constructed of **black basalt stone**. Most of the **marble** has since been scavenged for buildings elsewhere, partiularly in Denizli. South west of the Agora was the great **Arch of Domitian** built by the Proconsul Frontinus but the name of Domitian was later **removed** after his death when he was condemned by the Roman Senate for cruelty. To the north was located the large Roman Bath House and beyond it were the city latrine and the major necropolis of the city.

Above the city and to the east, Christians later constructed a large **martyrion/martyrium** to honor the **Apostle Philip** but his tomb had not been in the martyrion leading to **speculations** as to the legitimacy of such an earlier tradion and to the actual location of **Philip's tomb** until it was **discovered recently** down an incline, a short distance from the main structure. The hiddenness of the tomb was undoubtedly intended to protect it from the enemies of the early Christians.

[See Pictures # 97 and # 98 – Ruins of the Octagonal Martyrion (Memorial) to]
[the Apostle Philip and His Recently Discovered Tomb at Hierapolis]

Among the significant personalities associated with Hierapolis one must note the name of **Epictetus** (c.AD 60-120), who ultimately moved to Rome, was one of the leading Stoic

---

after he was married to the Theban princess Magara she caused him to to become crazy and he burned his house causing the death of his wife. Hercules went throrugh great anxiety for which he had to atone for his deed. Th Oracle at Delphi assigned him to Eurystheus, the King of Argos, who gave him 12 nearly imposible labors which he did and won immortality. Later he followed the pattern of his father Zues and when he cheated on his next love she arranged his death with a poisoned robe. His son Telephus, who was also a mighty warrior and by then was married to Hiera, became known as the founder of Pergamum.

Philosophers in the ancient world and whose work on ethics has often been compared to the thinking of Paul. As mentioned in connection with Laodicea and Colossae, Paul probably did not visit this region but the churches in the Lycus Valley were probably founded by **Epaphras** (cf. Col 1:7; 2:1; 4:13). **Papias**, who was the bishop of Hierapolis in the first third of the second century, is said in some sources such as Irenaeus to have been a friend of the martyr Polycarp and a disciple of the old man John who was a disciple of Jesus. But Eusebius citing the Preface to Papias' own work, *Exposition of the Oracles of the Lord*, disputes that Papias in fact had contact with the actual disciples of Jesus.[18] Nevertheless, the snipets we have from his writings in the works of others provide a strategic source for the Chritian traditions concerning the early church and our gospels.

Philadelphia/Alasehir: (37)
Philadephia was named for **Attalus II** who gained the nickname of "Philadelphus" (brotherly love) because of his commitment to his brother Eumenes II, the king of Pergamum. Typical of Roman patterns of **intrigue**, they tried to win the support of Attalus against his brother but he reufused those overtures and later succeeded him. Like the rest of the region it passed into Roman hands when it was bequeathed to Rome by **Attulus III** in 133 BC. Its history before the time of the Attalids is not clear but some early inscriptions may **suggest** that it may have served as a **Macedonian** outpost in the years preceding Pergaminian control.

Typical of the region, it was **subject to earthquakes** during this period and it was severely damaged in AD 17 from which it took a number of years to recover. Indeed, Strabo (*Geographica*, especially at xii.8.18 and xiii.14.10) mentions the severity of the quake and the aftershocks which necessitated the residents abandoning the city for a period of time until the tremors ceassed. Because of the assistance from Rome in granting reprieve by Emperor Tiberius from the payment of tribute during this period the city **redefined itself** as a "Neocaesarea" and followed a similar pattern of again being renamed as "Flavia" after the wife of Vespasian when he acted similarly in the devastating period following the earthquakes in 60 and thereafter. Lying on the Lydian and Phyrigian **frontier**, it was also subject to attacks from the people to the east -- a factor which may be linked to John's reference to the city as an **"open door"** (cf. Rev 3:8).

Because present city of Alasekir is built over the old city of Philadelphia **nothing much is evident** from the past except for some of the walls from the Byzntatine city, the pillars of arches from the Church of St. John the Theologian, some remnants of a stadium and archaeologists have uncovered some remains of a theater and temple on the old acropolis.

A short distance from Philadelphia (c. 10 miles/ 16 km) in the town of Ardabav was the headquarters of the early **Montanist movement**, a type of Pentecostal Christian movement that spread to various parts of the Roman Empire and to which the Latin writer Tertulian became attached.

---

[18] For some of these references see Eusebius, *Historia Ecclesiastica* iii.39.1-7. For convenience in respect to Eusebius and Codices Baroccianus and Coislinianus see Daniel J Theron, *Evidence of Tradition* (Grand Rapids: Baker Book House, 1958), 26-31.

Sardis/Sart/: **(38)** The city of Sardis lies about 30 miles (or a little less than 50 km) northwest of the city of Philadelphia/Alasehir and about twice that distance east of Smyrna/Ismir. It was the **capital** of the early **kingdom of Lydia** and the great fortress on the **acropolis** of one of the shelves of Mt. Tmolus was regarded as among the most defensible sites in the ancient world. In his attempted seige of this fortress, **Cyrus of Persia** was frustrated by its seeming invulnerability until, as the story goes, one of his soldieres in watching the fortress at night noticed that a helmet of a defender on the wall came crashing down to the slope below. Unaware that he was being observed, the defender soon emerged from a hidden entrance in the wall and retrieved his lost helmet. But the secret was revealed and the city fell to the Persians in 547 BC, thus ending the reign of Croesus and the Lydian Kingdom.

[See Picture # 99 – Temple of Artemis & the Historic Fortified]
[Acropolis at Sardis in the rear]

The message in the **Book of Revelation** concerning the coming of the Lord in the middle of the night must have reminded the readers of the way in which the city was taken at night (cf. Rev 3:3).

Our knowledge of the earlier city is **encrusted with myths** and folk-tales much like our understanding of early Heraklion in Crete. Indeed, the myths seem to overlap and may create confusion for the modern mind which seeks the security of order and logic. As one of the myths details, the **birthplace of Zeus** was thought by the residents of this area to be on Mt. Tmolus and they also added Dionysus to the story because the region is also known for its grapes and wines. As another story goes, the golden touch is here associated with **King Midas** (not Minos of Crete) who was understood to be a legendary king of Phyrgia and who sought to undo the curse of his miserly wish by bathing in the special waters of the Pactolus River. The point of this tale is obviously a reflection on the dominamce and the **early wealth** of the city and the region. It was also epitomized in the Mermnad kings, particularly Croesus, who **developed coins** as a **medium of exchange** and who thus encouraged the development of trade beyond the bartering system (cf. the **Minoans** who also developed a medium of exchange although it was in the form of **ingots**).

Another of the **fascinating Lydian stories** involves the end of the Heraclid dynasty which had ruled Sardis for about five centuries and the beginning of the Mermnad kings. According to the story, **Canadaules, the last of the Heraclids** was so proud of his wife's beauty that he challenged his assistant Gyges to hide in her bedroom and see her undress. Gyges finally acquiesced in the strange proposal but the queen saw him and because she had been compromised demanded that he either kill himself or kill the king and marry her. As one might guess, he chose to survive and replaced the king. The tale has of course been repeated by many writers from my point of view the **truth of it is questionable**. Instead, it appears to be a justification for a palace **intruigue** not verydifferent than the one among the aspiring Alexander Jannaeus and the crafty Salomi Alexander among the Hasmoneans in Israel.[19] Gyges ascended to the throne as a feared and powerful ruler. This **Gyges**, whose burial mound is a short distance from Sardis and who lived about the middle of

---

[19] For a discussion of Alexander Jannaeus and Salomi see Gerald Borchert, *Jesus of Nazareth*, 19-21.

the seventh century BC, is probably to be regarded as the **"Gugu,"** the nemisis of the ruthless Assyrians. It is also quite probable that this Gyges was the historical basis for the development of the strange apocalyptic evil figure in the Bible known as **Gog** and his nation known as **Magog** (e.g. the Mermnad dynastyof the north?) that Ezekiel predicts God will judge (Ezek 38:1--39:36) and which John pictures as the forces that will be aligned with Satan in challenging God but will be consumed by fire (Rev 20:7-10). Now in making these statements I must quickly add that it is highly unwise and indeed a fallacious pattern of interpretation to use such ancient apocaplyptic images as keys in attempting to identify contemporary people and nations as the figures intended in the ancient biblical texts. It just will not work because of all the subjective assumptions that are necessary. And with this statement I return to the discussion of Sardis per se.

Prior to the coming of the Persians, Herodotus indicates that **Croesus** the last and perhaps richest of the Lydian kings was concerned about the rising power of of the Persians and therefore consulted the **Oracle at Delphi**. He was told that if he crossed the Halys River beyond his kingdom that a great empire would be destroyed. Assuming the Oracle meant that he would destroy Persia , he went to battle and lost. Under **Persian rule** Sardis became the the **capital** of the western Anatolian frontier of a tightly integ rated Persian Kingdom and close ties were kept with Susa through the establishment of an **imperial road** system that ran eastward to the old Lydian boader and beyond to places like modern Ankara and then to Tarsus where it turned south through the Taurus Mountains into Mesopotamia through Ninevah to Susa. The Persian Empire continued to expand and even reached to the Aegean Islands which destined it to face Greece and ultimately Macdonia.

The **conflict with Greece** errupted early in the fifth century (499 BC) when the Ionian city states along the western coast of Anatolia rebelled against Persia and attacked Sardis with help from Athens. The Persians countered by mounting direct attacks on the Greek mainland under **Darius and his son Xerxes** which issued in a series of Persian-Greek wars but the Greeks were sustained both on land and at sea. While Athens was severely damaged, it was able to emerge from the battles into its glorious period with Pericles which did not last long because of the Peloponnesian Wars in Greece and the rise of Spartan influence. On the horizon, however, a new international force was emerging in Macedonia under Philip II and his son *Alexander G* which was destined to end the Persian Kingdom. The citizens of Sardis wisely recognized the power of the Macedonians and opened their gates to the marching forces of *Alexander G* in 334, thus preserving their city.

Following the death of *Alexander G*, the entire territory became the focus of a dispute between two of his generals (Lysimachus and Seleucus) and the **Selecids** conquered most of Anatolia, including Sardis and established it as their **western capital**, a distiction it maintained for about ninety years. During the reign of **Antiochus III** (the so-called Great), one of his generals, Achaeus, attempted to seize control of Asia which forced a response from Antiochus who after a seige of two years retook the city following the pattern of Cyrus. But the uprising caught the **attention of Rome** and in typical Roman fashion, it became involved in the issue siding with Eumenes II of Pergamum who claimed the territory. The outcome was predictable and Antiochus signed the Treaty of Apamea (188 BC) which gave Sardis and the rest of the entire region to Eumenes and the Attalid rulers.

When Attulus III died, he bequeathed his kingdom to Rome (133) and then Rome created the new Provicne of Asia from most of the aquired territory in 129 BC.

During the Roman period Sardis was established as one of the **major regional centers** in Asia and expanded greatly. But the severe **earthquake** that rattled the entire region in AD 17 also devestated Sardis. Emperor Tiberius responded to the disaster by providing a remission of duties and additional funds for the rebuilding of the city and it prospered in the following years, becoming one of the major cities of Asia even into the Byzantine period.

Because it was a strategic fortress guarding access to the sea from the east and to the northern areas around the Bosphorous, Sardis remained a target for enemies in the later Byzantine period, including: Persians from the south, Arabs from the southwest and Seljuks from the south and east. But the final nail in the coffin of Sardis as strong fortress and guardian against invaders came from farther east with the onslaught of **Mogols under Tamerlane** who literally vandalized and destroyed the city in AD 1402, leaving Constanitople/Byzantium much more vulnerable.

Visiting the site today is like walking through history where one can see various areas of habitation, worship and places of recreation. Consider: (1) the shells of some buildings like the magnificent **Imperial Marble Court** near **Gynmasium and Bathhouse** provide mute testimony to the existence of a once very thriving city; (2) whereas a short distance away the area of fallen columns in the vacinity of the **Great Altar** and the nearby **Temple of Artemis**, one of the largest Greek temples in the world where both Artemis and Zeus were both worshipped, give one the sense of an age long gone and some of the columns which are **embossed with the cross** remind one that the Christian faith had superseded the ancient cults that had once been honored at that place; (3) then walking down the **colonnaded street** and looking into the **little stalls** that once were busy places of business mostly of Jewish merchants gives one the erie feeling of wondering what will our cities look like in a thousand years; and (4) the lofty **Acropolis** with its **Fortress** which once was the symbol of protection and stability now merely stands abandoned and removed from the rest of the buildings on the plain, but -- **unlike at Pergamum --** only those who have time to spare are even tempted to climb the steep slopes in order to reach the former citadel. Of course, (5) there was a large theater (seating about 20,000) and a stadium/hippodrome nearby but these constructions are now denuded of their ancient marvels.

[See Picture # 100 - The Synagogue at Sardis which became a church]

At this point it is important to mention the fact that the **Jews** had been in region of Sardis for a number of centuries before the writing of Revelation. Aware of the traumatic years which the Jews faced under Persian domination during the time of Esther, many scholars now tend to identify the brief mention in **Obadiah 20** of the exiled Jews in **Sepharad** as a reference to the Jewish diaspora in Sardis. Moreover, many of the exiled Jews who lived in the lands of the Tigris and Euphrates were later forcefully **displaced by Antiochus III** from Mesopotamia to Anatolia, undoubtedly settling with fellow Jews in Sardis. Then during the time of Julius Caesar.in response to some Gentiles creating troubling unrest among the large Jewish population in Sardis, Josephus indicates that the procurator/praefect **Lucius Antonius** who served in Asia at the pleasure of Ceasar issued a special decree affirming rights granted to Jews in the province of Palestina and guaranteeing to the Jews of Sardis crucial **stated rights** and privileges, including: the right of synagogue assembly and of observing the Sabbath, the privilege to eat ancestral food, the right of self-government except in matters of state and the previously disputed right to contribute and send money to the temple in Jerusalem, rights which Josephus also reports were reaffirmed by Augustus (cf. *Antiquities* xiv.235; xvi171). Near the Gymnasium complex visitors today can walk through the remains of the large **Sardis Synagogue** with its beautiful marble floor and **Greek inscriptions** indicating that the community had become aculturized to Greek life. Among the other remains one can find surpising marble eagle and lion **sculptures** which may have been reused from a pagan source.

[See Picture #101 – An Ichthus Circle Revering Jesus as God's Son our Savior at Sardis]

The observant visitor can also discover indications from the time of transition when the synagogue was later used as a church (such as the ***ichthus*** symbol). During the second century AD, the leader of the Christian community , Bishop Melito, became embroiled in the early **Quartodeciman** argument over the dating of Easter. While the church of Sardis has virtually disappeared, the Orthodox Patriarch in Instanbul still maintains the metroplitan's seat but for all purposes he resides in Istanbul.

Pergamum/ Bergama: (39)

We now come in our circular visit to the last and most northerly of the seven church areas (mentioned as **third** after Ephesus and Smyrn) in the Book of **Revelation**. Pliny the Elder referred to Pergamum as "the most significant city in Asia" (*Naturalis Historia* v.126). While the later Hellenistic and Roman city became very expansive (which I shall try to explain later) the earliest evidences of settlement date from aound a thousand years before the coming of ***Alexandeer G***. The city basially owed its historical importance to **Lysimacus**, one of Alexander's generals who claimed Western Anatolia as his righful inheritance upon the death of his commander in Babylon. The intention of Lysimacus was the buiding and endowing of Pergamum and some other cities with the **vast treasure** roughly estimated at about 9,000 gold talents which he appropriated from *Alexander G*.

Unfortunately for Lysimacus his military colleague Seleucus who on the death of *Alexander G*. had taken as his disposition both Syria and Mesopotamia (although Ptolemy actual appropriated Israel) also wanted Western Anatolia as well. Accordingly, Lysimacus was forced by Selecus to engage in war. In marching away from Pergamum to do battle with Seleucus, he entrusted his fabulous treasure to **Philataerus,** his steward and one of his officers who was reputed to have been a eunuch. As Seleucus moved into Anatolia Philataerus, sensing the outcome of the war would be against Lysimacus, craftily shifted loyalties and when his former leader was killed, Philataerus immediately (281 BC) became very wealthy. He readily agreed to be the ruler of a small city realm within the Seleucid kingdom which continued to grow and he provided the Seleucids with a staunch ally in the north against invaders from further north and east. Since Philataerus had **no heirs**, he adopted his brother's sons, the eldest of which became Eumenes I in 263 BC who following the lead of his sponsor accelerated building construction in the city of Pergamum which naturally became the capital of the Attalid Kingdom. Eumenes was followed by his son **Attulus I** who declared himself a king and it is from him that the dynasty received its name. He successfully withstood an invasion from the Galatians or Celts for which he received the honorary designation of **"Soter"** (Savior).

Sensing the vulnerability of his little kingdom, Attulus forged an early **alliance with Rome** which in later years provided an important benefit to the city. His son, **Eumenes II**, reconfirmed this alliance but **Antiochus III** (the Great, the Seleucid strongman), recognized the danger which the allaiance with Rome meant to him and he sought by force to counter the growing strength of the Attalids by marching against them. This move definitely caught the attention of Rome and it naturally responded. The **Battle of Magnesia** (189 BC) proved to be unfortunate for Antiochus because the combined power of Pergamum and Rome was too much for him and he was force to aquiesse to the terms of the **Treaty of Apamea** (188BC) which delivered to Pergamum the Seleucid's important territories in Western Anatolia. This battle which apparently included the use of elephants by Acntiochus and the Antiochus'disgrace in the transference of his lands to Eumenes are also mentioned in **1 Maccabees 8:5-8** as a kind of divine judgment on the Seleucids who had been despotic rulers over the Jews.

During the reign of Eumenes II, Rome sensed a kindred spirit and allowed Pergamum additional authority over the Aegean area, even including Athens. Eumenes responded by constructing great monuments that including the magnificent **Altar of Zeus** in Pergamum, the largest in the ancient world measuring nearly 120 x 110 feet (36x30 m), which was removed from Pergamum by German archaeologists and is now housed in the state museum in **Berlin** (formerly called the Pergamum Museum but following the ensuing demand for its return by Turkey has been renamed). Also among his major construction projects was the beutiful **Stoa of Eumenes** in the Agora of **Athens** which has been carefully restored by American archaeologists.

Eumenes was succeeded by his brother Attulus II and then by Attulus III, the son, who was a weak ruler and his reign marked the decline and end of Attulid dynasty. By agreement with Rome, this nephew of **Eumenes II** on his death in 133 BC **bequeathed** the Attulid kingdom **to Rome**. But as one might expect, such a transfer was not accepted by all those in Pergamum and **Aristonicus** proclaimed himself to be in line for the throne as an illegitimate son of Eumenes II and he **laid claim** to the kingdom. In his effort to gain followers, he emancipated the slaves so that they could participate in the quest for freedom from Roman attachments. The ensuing three-year war with Rome proved to be hopeless for the Pergamese supporters of Aristonicus who was captured and executed. Rome then in 129 BC formed the new **Provine of Asia** from the Attalid kingdom.

Typical of Roman responses, although it granted Pergamum an **independent city** status because of its previous close relationship with Rome, it nevertheless imposed **heavy duties** on Pergamum for its rebellion and the Romans carried off its wealth so that during the uprising (89-84 BC) led by **Mithradates** VI of Pontus the proud Pergaminians readily joined in the ill-fated revolution and together with some of the other Asian cities **butchered** tens of thousands of **Roman citizens**. As might be expected, Rome cancelled Pergamum's favored status as a free city and severely taxed the residents which led to a major period of decline in the city.

But the fortunes of Pergamum began to change with the rise of Julius Caesar and especially with **Augustus**. In 29 BC it was granted the right to build the **first imperial temple** in Asia to Dea Roma and it honored Augstus as the soverign of the Empire. Its role as the **principal city** of Asia was reaffirmed until it lost its status as the capital of Asia to Ephesus at the end of the first century AD. Nevertheless, it remained a strong city that was endowed by both **Trajan and Hadrian** and honored with a temple in the honor of the Trajan and then linked to the second emperor as well. The city continued to grow in size and wealth during the second century, reaching its high point at about 150,000 during this period. And with the reconstruction of the famous Temple to Dionysus and rededicated for a short time to Caracalla it was in fact honored three times as a *neokoras* (imperial temple guardian) by Rome.

During the earlier period of expansion under the Attalids, Pergamum continually attracted intellectuals from various places around the Mediterranean and its library on the acropolis soon became a rival to the one in Alexandria. As the popular story goes, when Ptolemy and the Egyptians **refused** to send more **papyrus**, Eumenes and the Pergamese responded by developing their own writng material which was an early type of **parchment** from animal skins and which bore the Greek name of the city (*pergamum*). The truth is that this writing material had been in use in Asia for some time but it then became very popular because it was more durable than papyrus.

The **library** itself was a rather sophisticated building for its time with shelves on foundations that were not attached to the walls so as to allow the air to circulate around the scrolls and codecies. The number of resources in the library has been disputed because only about a tenth of the so-called 200,000 resources claimed to have been housed there would seem to fit the structure as we know it today. But politics also may allegedly also have played a hand in the fate of this library because after Julius Caesar unfortunately badly wrecked the famous library in Alexandria, Mark Antony, according to the story, stole many of the important holdings of the Pergamese library in order to pander Cleopatra, supposedly delivering them into her possession (cf. Plutarch, *Antonius* lviii.9 ff.). The truth of this story may be questioned.

The expansion and refurbishing of the medical centrer dedicated to Asclepius attracted well-known physicians including **Galen** and the great debater **Aelius Aristides** joined the rhetorical school. The city continued to attract students into the third and fourth centuries AD and among them was **Julian** (c.351) who later became the Emperor and was known as "the Apostate" because he rejected his earlier Chirsitan training, opposed it and turned instead to what today would be akin to a philosophical skepticism.

In the Footsteps of Paul and John

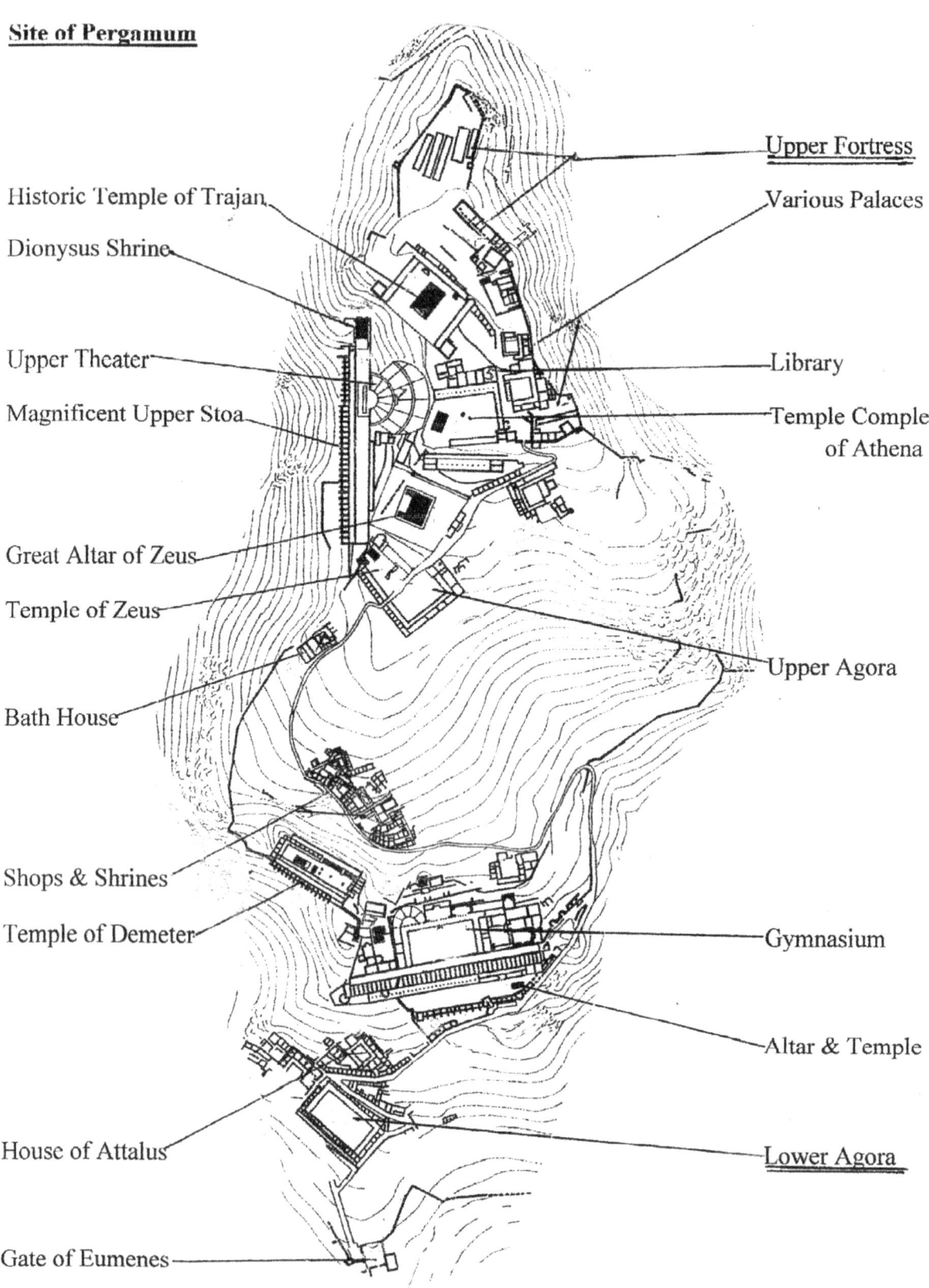

Site of Pergamum

The city suffered a series of attacks and lootings at the hands of the mauading Arabs after the time of Justinian. Thereafter, it was occupoied by various invading forces such as the Crusaders from Europe, the Seljuks from Mesopotamia and finally the Ottomans but none of them provided the basis for the city to regain its former glory. Today the sleepy modern town of Bergama which lies at the foot of the great acropolis mountain hardly compares to the city that once was the capitals of both the Attulid kingdom and the prestegeous Roman province of Asia.

The **primary ancient gods** revered here were **Zeus, Athena, Asclepius and Dionysus**, but others were also worhipped in this area. The most popular of these deities seems to have been Athena who was honored as *nikephoros* (the bearer of victory). The mention of Pergamum as the throne city for Satan (cf. Rev 2:14) has led to much speculation. Some have suggested that it may refer to the Altar of Zeus and others to the Asclepion where the medical images of the entwined snakes were evidnt. But certainty is not possible.

In comparison to Sardis, the Jewish population does not appear to have been large in this area since Cicero's reported seizure of the annual temple tax by Flaccus in AD 62 was rather small (*Pro Flacco* 68-69). While archaeologists have discovered a few evidences of a Jewish presence in the city, the synagogue has yet to be found.

The Book of Revelation indicates that there was a Chritian community in Pergamum by the end of the first century and Christian traditions have identified several believers who were **martyred** from Pergamum. Antipasis is mentioned in Revelation 2:13 but there are also traditions which include the names of Agathonice, Carpus and Paylus. Just as in the case of **Antipas**, however, not much is known concerning them or their actual times of death, although theories suggest that the latter three were killed in the reigns of Marcus Aurelius and/or Decius. Because of its significance as a city Pergamum became a **bishopric** in the second century and even today the Ecumential Patriarchy in Istanbul maintains a titular see for the city. Speculation continues concerning who were the Nicolaitans mentioned in Revelation 2:14.

Because Pergamum was a large city and since much of the area continues to be occupied today only portions of the ancient city have been excavated and most visitors will probably have the opportunity to see only portions of the extended sites. The most significant area is the **great Acropolis** but it too is expansive and located roughly on three levels. The top most level can be reached by a **gondola or cable tram** which saves one a very steep climb. The top of acropolis is normally windy but baring the onslaught of an unusual windy day in the winter season the lift will remain open. If it closes then the tourist bureau will provide taxis to the top, the ride up is fine but the taxi down can be likened to a nosedive into Hades. Fortunately very few visitors have such a pleasure (?) and frankly I do not wish to have it again.

[See Picture # 102 – Pergamum Foundation Passageway which once]
[supported the great buildings on the Acropolis]

In the Footsteps of Paul and John

Looking out from the **highest level of the acropolis** which rises nearly 1300 feet (400 m) about the valley floor is breathtaking. Here one finds primarily the remains of **Hellenistic** buildings including several **palaces** of Philataerus, Eumenes II and the Attalid rulers, the great **Library** and the historic **Temple to Athena** from the third century BC which bore the offerarory inscription "King Eumenes to Athena the bearer of victory" (now also in Berlin). In this sanctuary once stood a large statue of the goddess about 3 meters (10 ft) in height as well as a number of other votive offerings including the famous bronze statue of the **Dying Gaul** now in the Capitoline Museum in Rome which celebrated Pergamum's repeated victories over the invasions of these Gauls and especially of the triumph of Attulus I "Soter" over the Gauls. At the northern crowning point of the acropolis the Roman builders likely removed some earlier structures in order to erect what must have been a truly stunning **Temple in honor of Trajan** (later also linked to Hadrian and recognized Zeus), built on a grand terrace with its arched walkways and offering an incredible view of the entire area.

[See Picture # 103 – Pergamum Acropolis –Temple of Trajan]

To the south of these structures and at a slightly lower incline once stood the magnificent **Altar of Zeus** which was completely reomoved and is now in Berlin while just beyond the site of the altar was the **Upper/Acropolis Agora**.

Just in front of the temples, the library and the altar on a lower level is the **grand theater** built into the side of the cliff in the third century BC and modified several times. Its steep steps and eighty rows providing seating for about 10,000, together with its unusual portable stage setting and its exceptional **panoramic view of the valley** mark it as one of the most captivating theaters of the ancient world. Just in front and below the theater was a long **columned porch** or stoa running all the way from below the Temple of Trajan to the Upper Agora which provided a kind of **balcony** to the entire complex which overlooked the valley. As a testimony to the genius of the ancient builders, this Upper Acropolis in Pergamum must have rivaled the Acropolis in Athens for sheer magnificence and splendor!

Halfway down the acropolis slope there were located a number of shops and eating places the podium hall as well as a large **gymnasium complex** with several bathhouses and nearby were also several sanctuaries to other gods such as Demeter and Hera with an altar in the front of the complex. Lower down the slope there was a **Monumental Gate** dedicated to Eumenes II and above it was the Lower Agora and within this lower complex was a major house designated to Attulus.

In the city below the acropolis, built over the Selinus Biver is the huge **Red Hall**, constructed from red bricks and originally faced with marble, some of which remains in situ. On the eastern side of this temple complex were **two circular towers** which servered as smaller **temples** dedicated to **Egyptian gods** probably related to the various cults associated with the mysteries of Isis, of which we know very little. This inner temple section was primarily reserved for the priests. In the western portion of the temple section to which the devotees were allowed entrance, there once stood **an extremely large statue** of the god which was at least 10 meters (33 ft.) in height and which seems to have been **hollow** so that a priest could enter through a hidden tunnel and give various instructions, blessings or condemnations to the listeners. Further to the west was great enclosed **courtyard** for those waiting to attend the encounter in the temple area. This courtyard was surrounded on three sides by a colonnaded stoa, the columns of which were in the shapes of male (atlantes) and female (caryatid) figures. The circular temples later served as Christian chapels during the Byzantine period and the northern one has since been transformed into a mosque.

Some distance to the southwest of the acropolis is Pergamum's **famous Asclepeion**, enclosed on three sides by columned porches (stoa) with a bathing pool, sleeping accommodations, a **round temple** and a **larger round healing center** which was accessed though a special tunnel that must have given those in need of healing a sense of moving into an inner sanctuary. The entire complex was entered from the northeast through a columned **Sacred Way** that welcomed the visitor into the holy sanctuary of healing.

Especially like Ephesus, Aphrodisias and Hierapolis, the vestiges of ancient Pergamum offer Christian pilgrims some truly remarkable insights into the past which will long be remembered by visitors to this grand circle of the various cities encompssed within the region to which John originally addressed the Book of Revelation.

F. THE VACINITY OF ANCIENT TROY

In traveling north to the Dardanelles/Hellespont through the peninsula known as the Troad and on into Greece I must pause to reflect on several historic sites that are associated not merely with Paul but are also stamped deeply into ancient mythology and the history of the western world. While other places could be mentioned, I will pause at the sites of Assos, Troas and Troy before reaching Canakkale and the narrow channel of water that separates Asia from Europe.

Assos/Behramkale: **(40)** Traveling north from Pergamum along the Aegean coast one reaches the mountainous **peninsula** known as the **Troad**/Biga which juts out into the Aegean. Turning due west, one finally comes to the anient seaport city of Assos which lies across from the island of Lesbos. Assos may have been settled as early as the **tenth century BC** by Greeks from **Lesbos** and within 200 years it was the leading city of the peninsula but it gave up that status when Troas gained importance in Hellenistic times. The Lydians under **Croesus** of Sardis recognized its significance and conquered it at the beginning of the sixth century, only to give way to Cyrus and the **Persians in 546 BC**. It briefly gained its freedom from the Persians with the help of the Delian Confederacy of Greek cities but was retaken by Artabazus and the Persians in 477 and the ensuing period was a time of upheaval for those under Persian authority.

In the fourth century **Hermias**, a student of Plato, gained control of Assos and founded a **school of philosophy** in the city. After the death of Plato in 348 BC other philosophers joined him, among them were **Callisthenes, Theophratus and Zenocrates** and even the renowned **Aristotle** retreated here for three years following Plato's death. During this time in Assos Aristotle met and married Pythias, the adopted daughter of Hermias. The Persians returned in force, recaptured the city, killed

Hermias and Aristotle fled to Macedonia. The Persian control of Assos soon came to an end, however, with the rise of *Alexander G*.

As I have indicated repeatedly, the entire territory of western Anatolia quickly passed through the hands of Lysimachus and into Selecid control, beginning a new period of unrest. During this time of upheaval Cleanthes (331-232), one of the leading Stoics was born in Assos, went to Athens to study with Zeno and after the death of his teacher became the new leading voice for stoicism. The Attalids of Pergmum gained control of Assos in 241 and encouraged the rebirth of Greek ways for the next century. With the death of Attulus III in 133 BC, Assos along with the rest of \Western Anatolia was bequeathed into Roman hands and became part of the Roman provincial system.

As far as the site is concerned, today the area within the city walls and the acropolis along with the upper necroplis (cemetery) is usually designated by the Turkish name as Behramkale whereas th old fishing village below is normally identified as Assos. In this diescription, however, I will use name Assos for convenience. The high point of the acropolis where the sixth century BC **Temple of Athena** was located rises not quite 800 feet (240 m) above the seaport below but not much remains except the five full and about seven partial Doric columns which archaeologists were able to reset on the temple platform. The Hellenistic city including the acropolis was originally enclose with stout walls from the fourth century BC of which about half of the outer perimeter on the west is still standing along with most of inner acropolis wall. Near the acropolis is an early Ottoman mosque from the the fourteenth century AD. Below the acropolis and close to the western wall are the remains of the **Gymnasium** while below and nearer to the seaport is the main agora (both from the second century BC) and the **theater** with seting for at least 4,000 (probably from the third century BC). There is also near the theater the ruins of a Byzantine church which was probably constructed around the fifth century AD.

Assos was visited by the **Apostle Paul** on his return to Jerusalm during his **third major journey**. He came **overland** from Troas to Assos which was about 20 miles (32 km), while his companions came the longer way around choppy seas of the Troad penisula by ship. This division of the party has led to considerable speculation (Acts 20:13). Why did they leave him in Troas? Did he want to be alone? He spoke with the Christians in Troas for an extended time, so long in fact that Eutychus went to sleep and fell out of the window (20:9-10). Was Paul talking to them about his forthcoming imprisonment, as he did with the Ephesian elders in Miletus (20:17-35)? Did he need the time for reflection on the next stage of his life? Or was it just a matter of timing and his desire to stay in Assos as long as he could? And what did he do in Assos? These are **questions** that are worth contemplating. Moreover, we can ask how we might act, if we would face what Paul was expecting would happen to him?

Troas/Alexander Troas/Dalyan:

(41) Situated on the western coast of the Troad/Biga peninsula and protected from the stormy seas by the island of Tenedos/Bozcaada, Troas developed into an important artificaial seaport which in Hellenistic and Roman times became the guardian to the Hellespont/Dardanelles. It was founded as Antigonia around 310 BC by one of *Alexander G's* generals, **Antigonus** (the so-called *Monohpthalmos* because of his impaired vision) but the area was seized from him by **Lysimachus**, one of his military colleagues and renamed Alexandria. Since it was in the vicinity of the ancient city of Troy, it naturally became distinguished from the many other Alexandrias by appending the the ancient city's name to this new settlement. As it continued to develop in size and prestige, it surpassed Assos in importance, becoming the chief city of the Troad and the major divisional seaport in the northern Aegean for ships and trade headed either into the Hellespont and cities beyond or to Neapolis and the city of Philippi.

Troas became one of Rome's prized cities partly because the Romans traced their heritage back to Aeneas who according to legend came from the ancient city of Troy. It was a favorite of Julius Caesar and according to some unlikely folk-tales, he even thought about moving his capital there.[20] Augustus considered it along with Parium to be strategic in the defence of the Hellespont and gave it colonial status with all the privileges of Rome itself and endowing it with the name of *Colonia Augusta Troadensium*. It continued as a major center until Constantine founded his new capital at Constantinople in AD 330. At that point most shipping by-passed the city with the result that the port of Troas, like its earlier rival Assos, virtually became unnecessary and both of them then became encrusted with silt.

The site of Troas is quite large and now visible are significant parts of the **old city walls** which probably once stretched for at least 5 miles (8 km). Most of the site has been overgrown with weeds and other plants, although the initial stages of excavations have uncovered some important ruins. The foundations for the **Temple of Apollo** from the time of Augustus have been revealed as well as the Gymnasium and Baths of **Herodes Atticus** (c. AD 135), one of the great patrons of Athens who also was a patron of Troas, can be visited. The beginning of the **decumanus maximus**, the main east-west road, to the harbor has been uncovered as well. Also visible are the outlines of other buildings such as one of the odeions, a **Doric temple** and a large **theater** but much excavation work still needs to be done in order to reveal the full nature of the ancient city which at present is under soil and other deposits that are covering the remains.

Like many other people in his time, the **Apostle Paul** used Troas as his embarkation point for traveling between the Senatorial Provinces of Mysia/Asia and Macedonia, thus avoiding the once bandit invested areas of the Imperial Province of Thrace. His **first visit** to this area came after he had been turned away from going into both Asia and Bithynia and came through Mysia to the harbor city Troas where he received the **night vision to come to Macedonia** (Acts 16:6-9). As has been noted by many scholars, the first "we" sections of Acts begin at Troas and end at Neapolis and Philippi leading some to speculate on Luke's origin but one also needs to remember that when ship voyages are being recounted in ancient writings, they are usually in the first person plural. In 2 Corinthians 2:12-13 Paul mentions that he had a **fruitful ministry** ("an open door"), in Troas but because of his concern to meet Titus and learn how the Corinthians were doing he left for Macedonia and met him there. As indicated in the discussion of Assos, during his **third journey** on his way back to Jerusalem Paul stayed some seven days in Troas with the Christians there and during his evening discussion with them, he spoke so long that **Eutycius** went to sleep and fell out of the

---

[20] For a debunking of this folk-tale see Horace, *Carmina* (*Odes*) iii. 3.

window but Paul miraculously revived him and the people did not have to go into mourning while he was saying his "good-byes" to them (Acts 20:7-12). Later **Ignatius** was conducted through Troas to Neapolis and the Egnatian Road in Macedonia on his way to his marydom.

Troy/Truva/Trevfikiye: (42)

We now come to the ancient city of Troy, a name which is recognized by both scholars and school children alike and which has been seared into the history of the world because of **Homer's Illiad**. While the account of Homer is basically fictional, it has a sufficient foundation in history that it enabled **Heinrich Schliemann**, a German entrepreneur, to find the fabled city and carry off to Germany a number of precious artifacts, many of which have been subsequently lost during the wars of the twentieth century.

[See Picture #104 – Ruins of Ancient Troy]

Situated a short distance from its successor Troas, the later Alexander Troas (Alexandria near Troy), and not quite 20 miles (30 km) from the modern city of Canakkale on the Dardanelles/Hellespont, archaeologists have identified Troy with **nine periods** of settlement dating back as far as the **Early Bronze Age**, perhaps around 3000 BC. The settlement of Troy I probably runs from about 3000 to 2400 BC; Troy II +/-2400 to 2200 BC; Troy III to Troy V 2200 to 1700; Troy VI +/-1700 to 1250 and Troy VII +/- 1250 to 1000. Scholars debate which of the last two (**Troy VI or VII**) is most likely the time of the fall of Troy and the time imagined by Homer since an **earthquake** struck the city roughly about 1250 BC and would have greatly weakened its stout walls. Then following Troy VII the city apparently was basically left unrehabilitated for about three centuruies. Troy VIII was reconstructed as a Greek and Hellenistic city 700-100/85 BC then Troy IX became the Roman and Bizantine city which was honored by the emperors (100/85 BC to c.AD 500-600).

As Homer's well-known story goes, **Paris of Troy** abducted the exceedingly **beautiful Helen**, wife of Sparta's **Menelaus**, and carried her back to Troy. The Greeks/Mycenaeans under **Agamemnon**, the brother of Menelaus, followed in an effort to rescue her but the walls were too high and strong to be breached and failing in their early military efforts, they **devised a plan** to enter the city by building a huge **wooden horse** and hiding a contingent of soldiers inside it. Then pretending to sail away, the Greeks left the horse outside the walls. The Tojans became intrigued by the presence of the huge abandoned horse and assumed that it must have been left as a gift or for some other inexplicable reason and brought it inside the walls. At night the Greeks emerged and opened the gates to the Greek army that had been waiting in hiding and the doom of Troy was sealed. As I indicated above, the story makes excellent reading and it **probably** does reflect some type of an historical **conquest** of Troy around the **thirteenth or twelfth century BC**, although such a conquest is disputed by some.

Various Levels at the Site of Ancient Troy

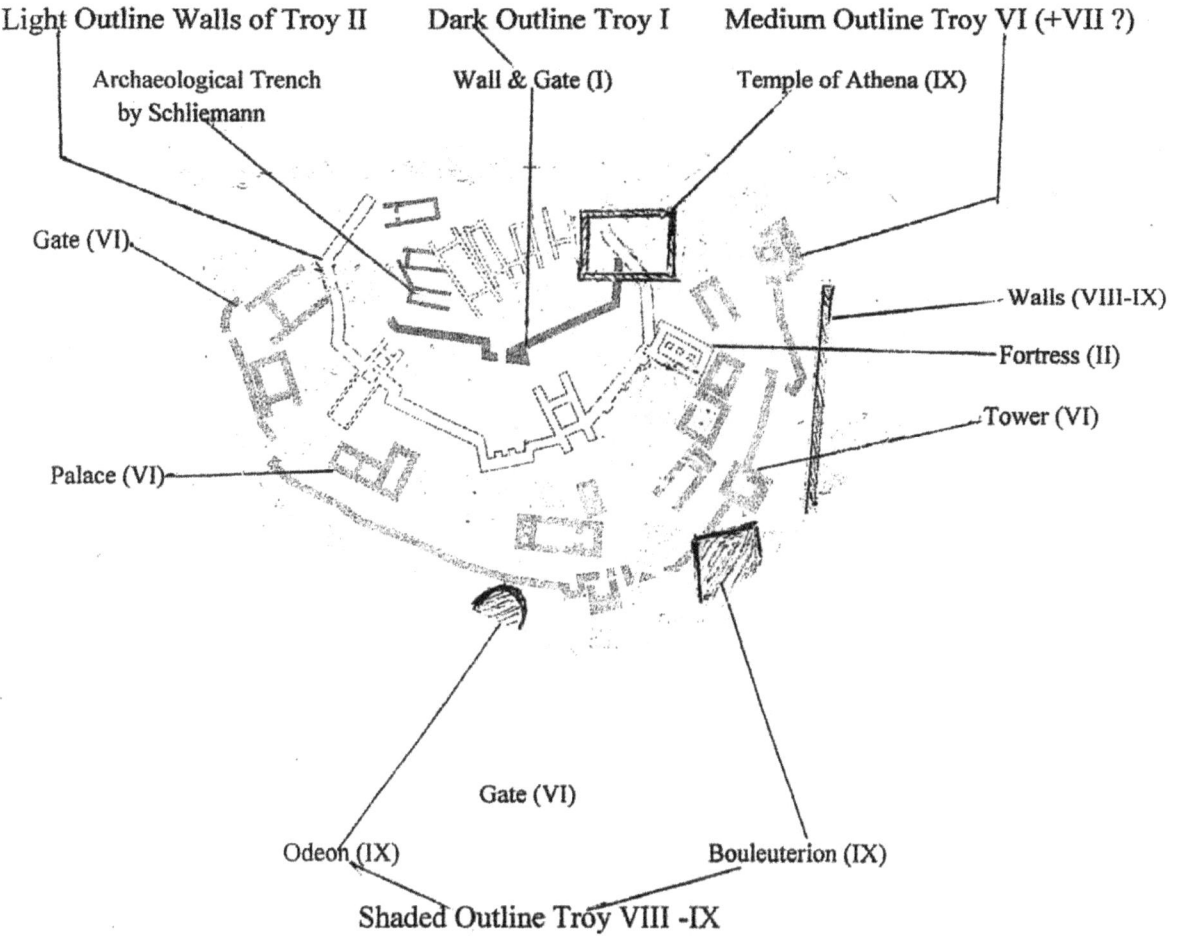

Visiting the **site** of ancient Troy can be a little **confusing** to those unfamiliar with understanding the archaeological work done on tels or mounds which have been built up over succeeding settlements. The layers have been marked by archaeologists but the problem is that in order to discern the relationship of the layers one has to have a **bird's-eye picture** of the removal of the layers and the fact that they are removed to different levels at different places. Seeing a model of the site before walking through the site can help a little and one must remember that when one moves through the site, one is actually going up and down through centuries of habitation. For example, the high point where the temple of Athena once stood is Troy IX while you enter from the stone steps into roughly Troy VIII and IX but as you go down the steps where you find red brick walls you are in the period as early as Troy II or III and beyond the temple you will find a the outline of walls and a gate that probably is from Troy I. Beyond the early trench of Schliemann one comes to the remains of the palace from Troy VI.

[See Picture # 105 – A Tourist Model of the Wooden Horse at Troy]

In the Footsteps of Paul and John

As you walk through the area, try to carry a site plan or remain close to your guide. When you finished your site visit, You will emerge from the area and enjoy taking a photograph of someone in your party who has climbed up the model of the **wooden horse** and is peering out one of the windows which has been prepared for tourists. Of course, if Homer's story has any historical viablikity, the horse would not have had windows and would have been much more akin to the movie version which can be seen on the promenade of the city of Canakkale which will be briefly discussed next.

Canakkale: **(43)** On the shore of the Dardanelles/Hellespont and opposite the Gallipoli Peninsula, the elongated **harbor city** of about a hundred thousand with a lively promenade is the overnight staging area for a return to Istanbul or for a journey on to the boarder town of Ipsala and Greece. The archaeological **museum** is small but has some fine items that are on display from both Assos and Troy. The most popular feature along the promenade is the **model** of the **Tojan Horse** that was constructed for the the 2004 movie about Troy.

Chapter 5

Some Helpful Information for Traveling to Greece and Turkey

Passports & Visas:

1. Be sure that your Passports are valid for at least six (6) months after you return.
2. Normally persons coming from Western Countries and many Asia Countries do not need Visas to enter Greece. A Visa is normally required of visitors to Turkey. A Visa Stamp should be purchased at the kiosk prior to passing through the immigration line. It is normally valid for 90 days. Check with your travel agent concerning who supplies the Visa. Arrival by Cruise ship at Kusadasi for a short visit to Ephesus will normally be handled by the company.
3. I advise people to make a photo copy of the two front pages of your passport and carry it with you in case something may happen to your important identification item. In many cases the guide in Turkey will request such a copy of this passport information because it is normally required when checking into the hotel.

Hotels:

1. Be sure to have your travel agent arrange for hotels for brief visits prior to arrival in Greece and Turkey. If you are traveling on your own by U-rail pass or by car, check with booking agents for rooms.

Guides & Drivers:

1. If you have a guide leading your tour, it is wise to request that the guide provide you with his/her cell phone number. Accordingly, if you become separated from your tour group, you will have a means of communication with the guide.
2. While tips are often included in tour packages, be prepared to offer both your guide and driver an appropriate gratuity. (I often recommend tour hosts collect about US$7.00-8.00 per day for their services to be divided at approximately 60% to 40%)

Medium of Exchange/Currencies:

1. The currency in Greece is the Euro. There has been a continuing debate in Greece concerning their participation in that currency and their debt level in comparison to Germany and France.
2. The currency in Turkey is the Lira. Turkey is struggling to be accepted into the Euro Zone.

3. Currencies can normally be exchanged at airports upon arrival in the countries being visited.

Protection of Money & Valuables:

1. It is important when traveling to protect your valuables and it is wise to leave your significant jewelry at home. Take jewelry you do not mind if it is lost.
2. For men, you may wish to carry your money credit cards and Passport(s) in a travel pouch under your shirt. Keep only a small amount of cash handy for making small purchases, food and tips.
3. For women, be sure to have a purse with a strap that you can hang around your neck and be sure that your purse has a zipper to ensure that it is closed.
4. Concerning Credit Cards, remember that Credit Card Companies now charge a fee for purchases made in a foreign currency even if the price is quoted to you in your own currency.

Electricity:

1. For those whose home appliances operate on 110 volts, remember to carry hair driers, razors, etc. which operate on 220 volts. Or carry a transformer along with the normal European 2 round prong plug adapter. Using a 110 volt appliance in a 220 volt line will burn out the appliance.

Dress:

1. Remember when you travel, it is wise to **dress in layers** so that you can add or subtract the layers according to the temperature during the day. This advice is crucial to being both comfortable and prepared for a variety of experiences.
2. Be sure that you are wearing comfortable shoes for travel, shoes that you have already broken in so that you do not raise blisters on your feet.
3. It is wise to carry flexible outer wear as well: for example a rain coat with a zipper lining provides for a variety of conditions. Some people carry a small folding umbrella in case of rain. Remember that Greece, especially has a variety of weather patterns and it is in the mountains which can see changes in the weather.
4. When entering Orthodox churches, shorts and bare shoulders sometimes are not accepted. Moreover, in Orthodox monasteries women should wear skirts which cover their knees. It is not necessary to wear a skirt to the monastery but a woman who does not have a skirt with her could then **carry a wide scarf** which she could wrap around her while in the monastery and then remove it when you exit the place. But do not worry if you have neither. Most of the monasteries are aware of this concern and have some scarves available for such purposes. This latter advice is particularly important if or when you visit the monasteries of Meteora in central Greece.

Packing/Luggage:

1. I advise all my groups to pack a change of clothing and two changes of underwear in your carry-on bag in the event that your checked bag is delayed. Moreover, I advise couples to place one set of the other person's clothing in their bag in case one bag is delayed and the other is not. It is always important to be as prepared as possible for unforeseen circumstances occurring when traveling.
2. Above all, **DO NOT pack your Passport or Medications in your checked baggage.**
3. Remember that larger bottles of **liquids** must be in the **checked luggage** and that smaller bottles (maximum 3 oz) of liquid and pastes (e.g. tooth paste) must be placed in a quart size plastic bag and displayed when passing through security with your **carry-on** luggage.
4. Take a notebook and a small Bible with you so that you can make notes concerning the pictures you take and the information that is new to you. I would, of course, also recommend that you carry this little travel book with you as you visit the various sites.
5. Remember **limits for checked baggage** on the airlines for those traveling in the general non-first class or non-business class seats. Do not exceed **50 pounds or 24 kilograms** because the fee is very high for long-distance travel. Moreover, for some airlines now the limit for basic tickets is **1 checked bag** on airlines such as Lufthansa. But Turkish Airlines still allows 2 checked bags. Note, however, that most tour companies pay for the portage of 1 bag in their agreements for land travel.
6. Be sure to use any baggage tags that your travel agents give you. They will help us to identify your bags en route at the airports and in the hotels for loading and unloading and getting the bags to your room. Also, put an identification card inside your checked baggage for additional idntification.

Cameras:

1. If your camera still uses film or disposable batteries, please make sure that you carry plenty of both. Most people take far more pictures than they had expected. If you use a chargeable battery, remember the electrical voltage issue.
2. My advice is not to carry expensive video equipment. But if you do, remember that in some countries you must register that equipment with customs as you bring it into the country. Check with your guide as you enter the country.

Food, Beverages and Water:

1. The foods in Greek and Turkish hotels and restaurants which are included in the visits on tours are safe and visitors should try the new foods. Of course, many of the desserts will be interesting and will be a delight.
2. Beverages are normally not included in meals and there is a charge for them.

In the Footsteps of Paul and John

3. Water is safe to drink in the hotels of Athens and Thessaloniki in Greece. I advise you to buy water in other places in Greece. I also advise you to by water throughout Turkey. Also, remember to **use bottled water for brushing your teeth!**

Shopping:

1. It is very important to mention this matter because most people are interested in taking back remembrances of their visits to places like Greece and Turkey. So the issue is one of balancing sight-seeing with shopping. Guides and tour directors know this tension and they want people to be able to engage in both. Let your tour guide and/or tour director know of your desires. They undoubtedly know the best places along the way where shopping can be accomplished and where your needs can be met, whether it is for tour books, pottery, jewelry, sweets and spices, leather goods, also many other items and of course some may want to see carpets in Turkey, even if they do not have the money. But try to be sensitive to the wishes of everyone who is traveling with you. And please give heed to the next and final category in this brief statement concerning information for traveling in Greece and Turkey.

Schedules/Time:

1. Remember that keeping on **time is absolutely crucial** to a great visit in Turkey and Greece. Getting up on time and being on the bus at the scheduled time is important and then returning to the bus promptly at the designated time after a visit to a site is significant if you wish to see all that is planned on the schedule. I have left this item for last because of its importance to your guide and tour director who will want you to see as much as possible.

May you have a Great Visit to these important lands of our Christian Heritage. As you walk where the Apostles walked and proclaimed their faith in the Risen Lord to a pagan world may you also be inspired to renew your commitment Jesus Christ. And may you return to your home with a new vitality for reaching out to others who need to know the promise of new life in him. God bless you!

Cordially in Christ

Gerald L Borchert, Ph.D.

A BRIEF BIBLIOGRAPHY

The following books represent some suggestions for further study and consultation.

Ancient Authors:

Ford, James H., Ed. *Homer, The Iliad and Odyssey: the Greek Classics*. Translated by Barton Williams. El Paso, TX: Norte, 2005 [A helpful introduction].

Homer, *The Iliad*. Translated by William F. Wyatt. Books I-XII, XIII-XXIV. In the Loeb Classical Library. Cambridge MA: Harvard University Press, 1924-25. [Loeb L 170-71.]

_____. *The Odyssey*. Translated by A. T. Murray. Books I-XII, XIII-XXIV. In Loeb Classical Library. Cambridge, MA: Harvard University Press, 1919-1995. [Loeb L 104-05.]

Pliny, *Natural History*. Translated by H. Rackham, et al. Books I-XXXVII In the Loeb Classical Library. Cambridge, MA: Harvard University Press, 1938-1962. [Loeb L 330, 352-53, 370-71, 392-93, 418, 394, 419.]

Strabo, *Geography*. Translated by H. L. Jones. Books I-XVII. In the Loeb Classical Library. Cambridge, MA: Harvard University Press, 1917-1932. [Loeb L 049-50, 182, 196, 211, 223, 241, 267.]

Tacitus, *Histories*. Translated by John Jackson. Books I-XVI. In the Loeb Classical Library. Cambridge, MA: 191925-1931. [Loeb L 035, 111, 249, 312, 322.]

Some Works on Mythology:

Apollodorus. *The library of Greek Mythology*. Translated by Robin Hard. In Oxford World Clasics. Oxford: Oxford University Press, 1997.

Hard, Robin. *The Routledge Handbook of Greek Mythology: Based on H. J. Rose's Handbook of Greek Mythology*. London and New York: Routledge, 2003.

Also see:

Evslin, Bernard. *Heroes, God's and Monsters of Greek Myths*. New York: Dell Laurel Leaf/Random House, 1984 [A simple introduction].

Napoli, Donna Jo and Christina Balit. *Treasury of Greek Mythology; Classic Stories of Gods Goddesses, Heroes and Monsters*. In National Geographic Books. Washington, DC: National Geographic, nd.

A Few Other Sources you may wish to consult:

Barrett, C. K. *The New Testament Background: Selected Documents*. New York: Harper & Row, 1961.

Borchert, Gerald L. *Jesus of Nazareth: Background*, Witnesses and Significance. Macon, GA: Mercer University Press, 2011.

_____. "Revelation." In *NLT Study Bible*. Carol Stream, IL: Tyndale House, 2008.

Bromiley, Geoffrey W., et al., eds. *The International Standard Bible Encyclopedia*. Vols. I-IV. Fully Revised. Grand Rapids, MI: William B. Eerdmans, 1979-1988.

Cook, S. A., et al., eds. *The Cambridge Ancient History*. Vols. XI-XII. Cambridge: University Press, 1936-1939.

Dubin, Marc. *Greece: Athens and the Mainland*. In Eyewitness Travel Guides. London and New York: Dorling Kindersley, 2003.

Fant, Clyde E. and Mitchell G. Reddish. *A Guide to Biblical Sites in Greece and Turkey*. Oxford and New York: Oxford University Press, 2003.

Hemer, Colin J. *The Letters to the Seven Churches of Asia in Their Local Setting*. In Journal for the Study of the New Testament, Supplement Series 11. Sheffield, England: JSOT Press, 1986.

Latourette, Kenneth Scott. *A History of Christianity*. New York: Harper and Brothers, 1953.

Malina, Bruce J. *The New Testament World: Insights from Cultural Anthropology*. Atlanta: John Knox Press, 1981.

Meeks, Wayne A. *The First Urban Christians: The Social World of the Apostle Paul*. New Haven: Yale University Press, 1983.

Mehling, Franz E., et al. ed., *Greece: A Phaidon Cultural Guide*. Englewood Cliffs, NJ: Prentice-Hall, 1985.

Perowne, Stewart. *The Journeys of St Paul*. London: Hamlyn House, 1973.

Sherwin-White, A. N. *Roman Law and Roman Society*. Oxford :University Press, 1963. Reprinted Grand Rapids: Baker, 1992.

Wilson, Mark. *Biblical Turkey: A Guide to the Jewish and Christian Sites of Asia Minor*. Istanbul: Ege Yayinlari, 2010.

PICTURES: FROM THE GREEK MAINLAND

1 a & b. The Bema near *Via Egnatia*, the Philippi Forum, & the sign for the ancient highway

2. Traditional Site of Paul's Imprisonment 3. The Grand Theater in Philippi

4. The Baptismal Park at Philippi 5. The Lion of Amphipolis

6 a. The White Tower in Thessaloniki and

6 b. Mount Olympus from the the White Tower

7. The Basilica of St. Demetrius

8. Statue of Dionysus – Thessaloniki Museum

9. The Roman Forum in Thessaloniki

10. The Memorial to Paul at Beroea

11. The Union of Bones in the Grand Meteoron

12. One of the Historic Monasteries in Meteora

13. St. Stefanos Monastery at Meteora

14. The Ruins of the Temple of Apollo at Delphi

15. The Navel of the World at Delphi

16. The Treasury of Athens at Delphi

17. The Picturesque Theater at Delphi

18 a & b. The Famous Charioteer and Philosopher Statues in the Delphi Museum

In the Footsteps of Paul and John

19. The Stadium/Hippodrome in Delphi

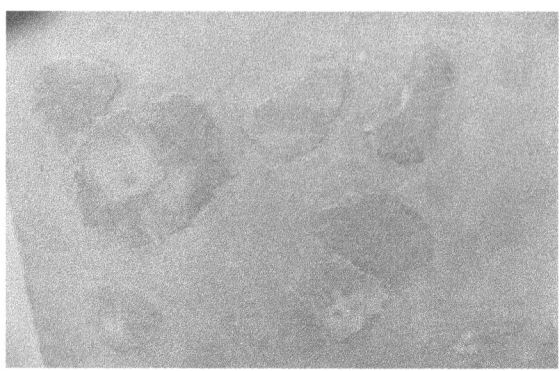

20. Inscription Concerning Gallio at Corinth in the Delphi Museum (cf. Acts 18:12)

21. The Acropolis of Athens at Night

22. Acropolis from the Odeon of Herodes Atticus

23. Theater of Dionysus from the Acropolis

24. The Asclepion from the Acropolis

25. The Areopagus (Mars Hill) from the Acropolis

26. The Sacrosanct Double Temple Erecthion Dedicated to Both Poseidon (left) Athena (center) with the Celebrated Caryatid Porch (far right)

27. Original Caryatids in the Acropolis Museum 28. The Caryatid Porch of the Erecthion

29. Frieze from the Parthenon in the Museum 30. The front of the Parthenon

31. Temple of Hephaistos in the Agora wrongly known as the Thesion)

32. Stoa of Attalus in the Agora (Sometimes (Reconstructed by American Archaeologists)

33 a, b, c. National Archaeological Museum Artifacts: Gold Death Masks, the young Rider and (below) Aphrodite being tempted by Pan and the flying Eros.

34. Bronze Statue of Augustus - who became the Pontifix Maximus in 12 BC.

35. The Corinthian Canal

36. The Temple of Apollo in Corinth

37 a & b. The Bema where Paul stood before Gallio in Corinth & the Arocorinth with the HistoricTemple of Aphrodite at the top in the background (Acts 18:12)

38. Inscription of Jewish Synagogue (cf.Acts 18)

39. Replicas of Body Parts Recovered from from the Asclepion in Corinth

40 a & b. The Grand Entrance with the Huge Lion Gate Stone to Ancient Mycenae

41 a & b. The Royal Burial Circle at Mycenae

42. The Best Preserved Ancient Greek Theater at Epidarus

PICTURES: FROM THE GREEK ISLANDS

43. Mykonos Harbor

44. The Windmills of Mykonos

45. Monastery of St. John on Patmos

46. The Famous Bell Tower on Patmos

47. Entrance to the Grotto – Traditional Site where John Received the Visions for the Apocalypse

48. A Fresco of John on the wall of the Grotto

49. Harbor at Rhodes (Site of the Colossus ?)

50. The Gigantic Fortress of Rhodes

51. and 52. Two Facades of the Crusaders Nations (Hostels/Tongues) in Rhodes

53. Acropolis at Lindos on Rhodes

54. St. Paul's Harbor at Lindos

55. Scores of Shops line the Streets in Rhodes   56. Copies of Ancient Pottery on Sale

57. and 58. Restorations of the Palace and Royal Chambers at Knosos in Heraklion (Crete)

59. Palace Sophisticated Cooling System   60. Royal Bull, Symbol of Minos and the Minoans
(Also related to Zeus and the Ancient Myths)

Gerald L. Borchert

61. Refurbished Throne Room in the Palace   62. Large Storage Jars for grain, olive oil and wine

63. and 64. Memorial Minoan Axe Heads and Minoan Currency in the Archaeological Museum

65. Statues which reflect the Great Myth concerning the Abducted Persephone (left); Pluto -- the god of the Underworld (right); and the Three-headed Dog, Cerberus, the guardian of Hades (center)

66. Anchored in the Volcanic Bay of Thira/Santorini

67. The Gondola for Ascending the Volcano's Wall   68. A View of the City and the Bay

69. and 70. The Beautiful Orthodox Church and its Interior on the top of Santorini

Gerald L. Borchert

PICTURES: FROM WESTERN TURKEY

71. The Modern Harbor City of Kusadasi

72. Statue of Artemis (Diana) in the Museum at Ephesus

73. The Famous Library of Celsus at Ephesus

74. An Imperial Temple at Ephesus

75. An Ancient Footprint – Sign of a Brothel

76. The Great Theater of Ephesus and the Colonnaded Way

77. Niki (Victory) holding a Wreath & Palm Branch -- Ephesus – 78. Entrance to the Civic Agora

79. Paul flanked by Theca and her Mother in a Recently Discovered Cave above Ephesus/Ayasoluk
80. The Basilica of St. John in Ephesus/Selcuk

81. *Hagia Sophia:* Justinian's Christian Cathedral 82. The Third Court of the Topkapi Palace
- -Byzantium/Constantinople/Istanbul-

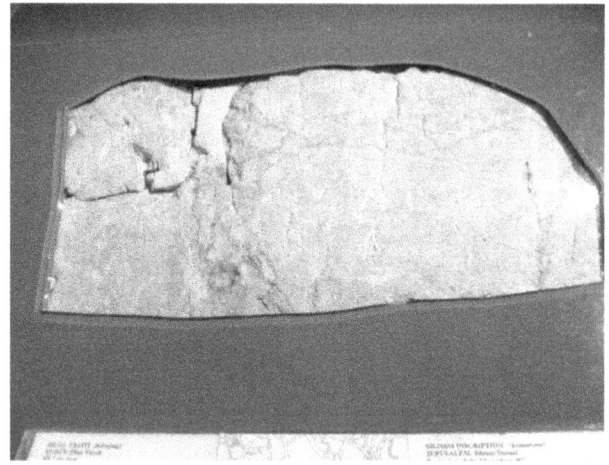

83. The Blue (Sultan Ahmet) Mosque

84. Museum Inscription from Hezekiah's Tunnel

85. and 86. Artifacts from Ancient Babylon and Sumer in the Istanbul Archaeology Museum

87. The Spice Bazaar of Istanbul

88. The Majestic Fortress on the Bosphorus

89. The Theater and Civic Agora at Aphrodisias

90. A Section of the 30,000 seat Hippodrome

91. Ruins of the Temple of Aphrodite

92. Frieze of Aphrodite in the Museum of Aphrodisias

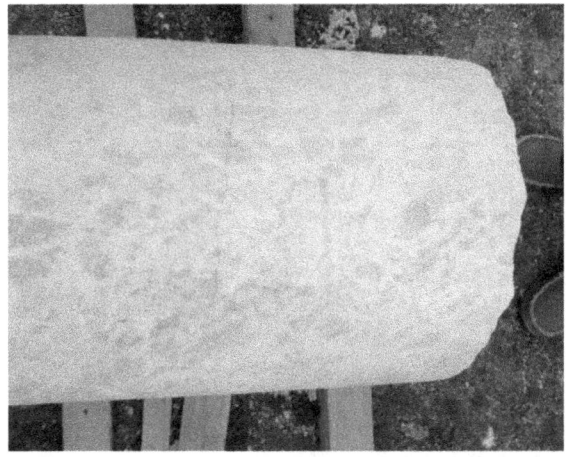
93. The Laodicean Temple of Artemis was changed into a church

94. Partly Reconstructed Temple and the Central Agora at Laodicea

94. Remains of the Western Theater of Laodicea

96. The Famous White Calcified Cliffs of Hierapolis -- Pamukkale ("Cotton Castle")

97-98. Ruins of the Octagonal Martyrion (Memorial) to the Apostle Philip and His Recently Discovered Tomb at Hierapolis

99. Temple of Artemis & the historic Fortified Acropolis at Sardis in the rear

100. Synagogue at Sardis - became a church

101. An *Ichthus* Circle Revering Jesus as God's Son our Savior at Sardis

102. Pergamum Foundation Passageway supporting the buildings on the Acropolis

103. Pergamum Acropolis –Temple of Trajan)

104. Ruins of Ancient Troy

105. A Tourist Model of the Wooden Horse at Troy

INDEX TO PLACES AND PICTURES

(The Numbers in **Bold Face** associated with sites are KEYED to BOTH the MAPS and the DISCUSSIONS in this book. The **bold small** letters relate to the map of Mainland Greece. The numbers in the normal print represent the STARTING page where the SITE is DISCUSSED. The Pictures related to the places are in square italic brackets *[ ]*)

Aigai – see Vergina

Akisar – see Thyatira

Alasehir – see Philadelphia

Alexandria Troas – see Troas

Amphipolis – **2** / p. 21/ *[p. 109]*

Aphrodisias/Afrodisias/Geyre – **33** / p. 80/ *[p. 129]*

Apollonia – **a** / p. 22

Assos/Behramkale – **40** / p. 97

Athens (see also Piraeus) – **9, 20** / p. 32/ *[pp. 114-17]*

Ayasoluk – see Selcuk

Balet – see Miletus

Balikesir – **28** / p. 74

Behramkale – see Assos

Berea/Breoea/Veria – **5** / p. 26/ *[p. 110]*

Bergama – see Pergamum

Bursa/Prusa – **27 /** p. 73

Byzantium/Constantinople/Istanbul – **23** / p. 64 and 137/ *[pp. 127-28]*

Canakkale – **43** / p. 102

Cenchrae – **10** / p. 40

Chalcedon/Kadikoy – **24** / p. 71

Colossae/Honaz – **35** / p. 84

Constantiople – see Byzantium/Istanbul

Corinth & Cenchreae & Lechaion/Lechaeum – **10** / p.40/ *[pp. 118]*

Crete – **18** / p. 53/ *[pp. 122-23]*

Daylan – see Troas/Alexander Troas

Delos – **13b** / p. 50

Delphi/Delfi – **8** / p. 29/ *[pp. 112-14]*

Ephesus also Ayasoluk/Selcuk – **14, 22** / p. 60/ *[pp. 125-27]*

Epidarus – **12** / p. 45/ *[p. 119]*

Eskihsar – see Laodicea

Geyre – see Aphrodisias

Gullubache – see Priene

Heraklion/Knossos (on Crete/Kriti) – **18** / p. 53/ *[p.122-23]*

Hierapolis/Pumukkale-"Cotton Castle" – **36** / pp. 85/ *[pp. 130-31]*

Honaz – see Colossae

Istanbul – see Byzantium/Constantinople

Izmir – see Smyrna

Izmit – see Nicomedia

Iznik – see Nicea

Kusadasi – **21** / p. 60/ *[p. 125]*

Laodicea/Eskihsar – **34** / p. 81/ *[pp.129-30]*

Lechaion – **10** / p. 40

Lindos (on Rhodes) – **17** / p. 52/ *[p. 121]*

Meteora (Kalambaaka) – **7** / p. 28/ *[p. 111]*

Miletus – **32** / p. 78

Mount Athos – **b** / p. 23

Mount Olympus – **c** / p. 25/ *[p. 110]*

Mycenae/Mycene/Mykine – **11** / pp. 44/ *[p. 119]*

Mykonos – **13a** / p. 50/ *[p. 120]*

Neapolis, Kavalla – **4** / p. 21

Nicea/Iznik – **26** / p. 72

Nicomedia/Izmit – **25** / p. 72

Olympia – **d** / p. 45

Pamukkale – see Hierapolis

Patmos – **15** / p. 50 / *[p. 120]*

Pergamum/Pergamon/Bergama – **39** / p. 91/ *[p. 132]*

Philadelphia/Alasehir – **37** / p. 87

Philippi – **3** / p. 18/ *[p. 109]*

Pireaus **20 and 9 /** p. 49

Priene/Gullubace – **31** / p. 77

Prusa – see Bursa

Rhodes/Rhodos – **16** / p. 52 / *[pp. 121-22]*

Saloniki – see Thessaloniki

Santorini/Thira – **19** / p. 57 / *[p. 124]*

Sardis/Salhili/Sart – **38** / p. 88 / *[p. 131]*

Selcuk/Ayasoluk also Ephesus – **22** / p. 60, 63/ *[p. 127]*

Smyrna/Izmir – **30** / p. 75

Sparta – **e** / p. 46

Thessaloniki/Thessalonica/Saloniki – **1** / p. 23/ *[p. 110]*

Thyatira/Thyateira/Akhisar – **29** / p. 74

Troas/Alexander Tros/Daylan – 41 / p. 98

Troy/Truva/Tevfikiye – **42** / p. 100

Vergina/Aigai – **6 /** p. 26

In the Footsteps of Paul and John

INDEX TO AREA AND SITE MAPS

AREA MAPS

Changes in the Roman Empire – p. 16

Mainland Greece – p. 17

The Greek Islands – p. 49

Western Turkey/Anatolia – p. 59

SITE MAPS

Ancient Athenian Acropolis – p. 36

Ancient Corinth – p.42

Ancient Delphi – p. 30

Ancient Ephesus – p. 62

Ancient Pergamum – p. 94

Ancient Philippi – p. 19

Ancient Troy – p. 101

The Golden Horn of Istanbul – p. 137

The Golden Horn of Istanbul

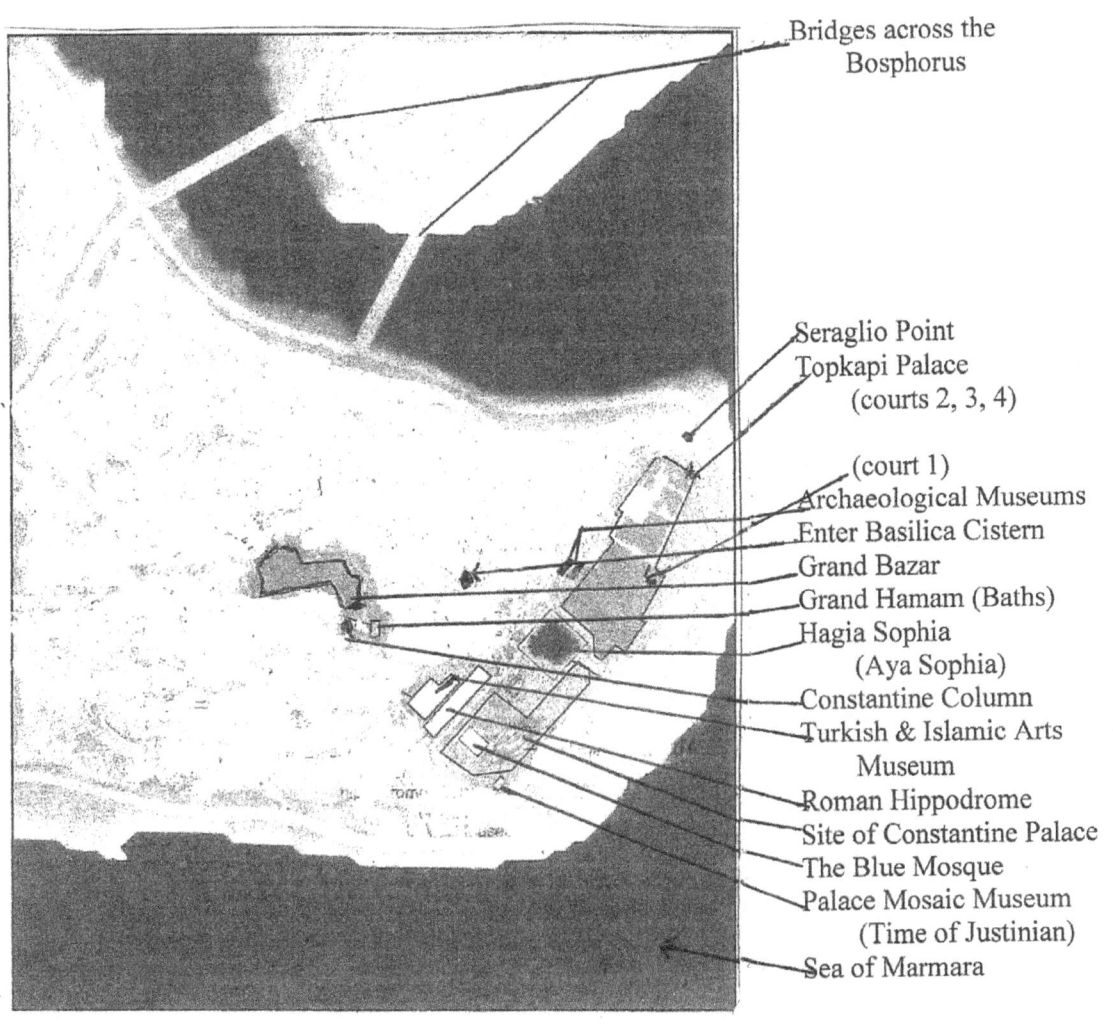

www.ingramcontent.com/pod-product-compliance
Lightning Source LLC
Chambersburg PA
CBHW080515110426
42742CB00017B/3125